Basic Beadweaving: Herringbone Stitch

Compiled by Julia Gerlach

Printed in the United States of America

05 06 07 08 09 10 11 12 13 14   10 9 8 7 6 5 4 3 2 1

Publisher's Cataloging-In-Publication Data
(Prepared by The Donohue Group, Inc.)

Basic beadweaving : herringbone stitch / compiled by Julia Gerlach.

  p. : ill. ; cm.

  ISBN: 0-87116-235-0

1. Beadwork--South Africa--KwaNdebele. 2. Beadwork--Patterns. 3. Jewelry making. I. Gerlach, Julia. edt II. Title.

TT860 .B37 2005
745.58/2

Senior art director: Lisa Bergman
Book layout: Sabine Beaupré
Photographers: Bill Zuback, Jim Forbes
Project editors: Julia Gerlach, Pam O'Connor

Acknowledgements: Mindy Brooks, Terri Field, Lora Groszkiewicz, Kellie Jaeger, Carrie Jebe, Diane Jolie, Patti Keipe, Alice Korach, Tonya Limberg, Debbie Nishihara, Cheryl Phelan, Carole Ross, Candice St. Jacques, Maureen Schimmel, Kristin Schneidler, Lisa Schroeder, Terri Torbeck, Elizabeth Weber, Lesley Weiss

CONTENTS

HOOKED ON HERRINGBONE

Contemporary beaders draw upon the traditional stitches of many cultures, adapting them for new applications and revising them to suit the contours of modern design. Recently, the herringbone stitch, originated by the Ndebele (EN-duh-bel-ly) tribe of South Africa, has gained a higher profile in Western beadwork. Many beaders are attracted by its supple drape, unique texture, and the relatively speedy progress its two-bead-per-stitch technique permits.

This book surveys a full array of herringbone projects—from a sleek basic bracelet to an intricate floral necklace that reveals the stitch's remarkable flexibility. Each of the book's three sections focuses on one aspect of the stitch. The first section explores flat herringbone and culminates in a dazzling collar created by artist Carole Horn. The second section looks at tubular herringbone, delving into the many permutations of herringbone rope in current beadweaving design. The third section, "Variations and combinations," embraces several versions of the stitch as well as many ways to combine it with other techniques.

Each section is supported with a page or more of beading basics that explain all the essential techniques needed to complete the projects. And every project contains the hallmarks of a *Bead&Button* how-to article—precise instructions, helpful how-to photographs and figures, detailed materials lists, and the confidence that the projects have been tested by our editors.

If you're new to herringbone, these projects will have you hooked in no time. And for those who are already herringbone aficionados, inspiration awaits!

THREAD AND KNOTS

CONDITIONING THREAD
Conditioning straightens and strengthens your thread and also helps it resist fraying, separating, and tangling. Pull unwaxed nylon threads like Nymo through either beeswax (not candle wax or paraffin) or Thread Heaven to condition. Beeswax adds tackiness, which is useful if you want your beadwork to fit tightly. Thread Heaven adds a static charge that causes the thread to repel itself, so it can't be used with doubled thread. All nylon threads stretch, so maintain tension on the thread as you condition it.

HALF-HITCH KNOT
Come out a bead and form a loop perpendicular to the thread between beads. Bring the needle under the thread away from the loop. Then go back over the thread

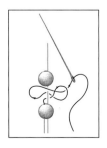

and through the loop. Pull gently so the knot doesn't tighten prematurely.

SQUARE KNOT
1 Cross the left-hand cord over the right-hand cord, and then bring it under the right-hand cord from back to front. Pull it up in front so both ends are pointing upward.

2 Cross right over left, forming a loop, and go through the loop again from back to front. Pull the ends to tighten the knot.

SURGEON'S KNOT
Cross the right-hand cord over the left-hand cord, and then bring it under the left-hand cord from back to front. Go over and under again. Cross the left end over the right end and go through once. Pull the ends to tighten.

FLAT HERRINGBONE

Flat herringbone basics

Herringbone stitch is characterized by columns of beads that tilt toward each other, creating a pattern that looks like the ribs of a herring. Each column of beads is referred to as a stack. Virginia Blakelock introduced herringbone to American beaders in her seminal book on beadweaving, *Those Bad, Bad Beads*. She taught it with what has become known as the traditional start, which allows the base row of beads to line up in the herringbone pattern. Many beaders have since adapted the stitch to start with a bead ladder, though this approach stabilizes the base row and prevents it from lining up in the herringbone formation. Most of the projects in this book begin with a ladder, though Carole Horn's "Rainbow collar," p. 18, begins with the traditional start. For simplicity's sake, only the ladder start is presented here, with the traditional start taught within Carole Horn's project.

FLAT HERRINGBONE, BEGINNING WITH A LADDER

While herringbone projects can be started with any number of beads, the most straightforward approach involves beginning with an even number. Begin by making a bead ladder, as follows, and then switch to herringbone stitch in row 2.

1 Thread a needle with 2 yd. (1.8m) of beading cord. Pick up two beads. Leave a 3–4-in. (7.6–10cm) tail and go through both beads again in the same direction. Pull the top bead down so the beads are side by side. The thread exits the bottom of the second bead. String a third bead and go back through the second bead from top to bottom. Come back up the third bead.

2 String a fourth bead. Go through the third bead from bottom to top and the fourth bead from top to bottom.

Add odd-numbered beads like the third bead and even-numbered beads like the fourth.

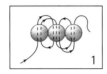
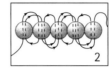

3 To stabilize the ladder, zigzag back through all the beads.

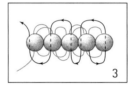

4 To begin row 2, pick up two beads and go down through the second ladder bead. Come back up the third ladder bead and repeat until the second row is complete.

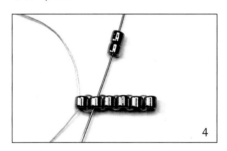

5 To make the turn and begin the next row, exit the last bead of row 1, string one or more accent beads, and come back up through the last bead of row 2. The accent beads are used to cover the thread between rows. Begin row 3 like row 2. When the working thread is about 6 in. (15cm) long, end it and add a new thread.

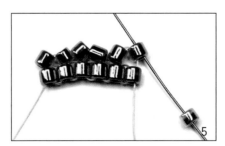

ADDING AND ENDING THREAD

Thread the needle on the tail end of your new piece of thread. Insert the needle in the bead from which the old thread exits and go down four beads (a–b). Go up three beads in the adjacent stack (b–c). Go down two beads in the first stack (c–d). Go up three beads in the second (d–e). Go down four to six beads in the third (e–f). Then trim the short tail off and thread the needle on the long end. Follow a similar path to end the old thread.

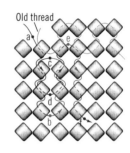

Old thread

Basic bracelet

a

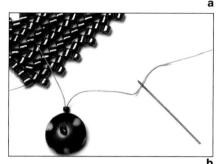
b

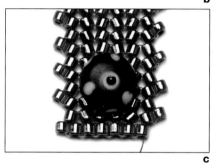
c

A bracelet made with relatively large beads is a good first project if herringbone is a new stitch for you. To spice up the basic design, intersperse sparkling crystals among the seed beads for a portion of the band.

MAKE THE BAND

❶ Determine how long you want your bracelet to be. The length depends on the number of seed bead rows on each end. For a 6½-in. (16.5cm) bracelet you will need about 16 rows on each side. For each additional ½ in. (1.27cm) in length add 3 rows to each side.

❷ Thread a needle with 3 yd. (2.7m) of Fireline. Leaving a 10-in. (25cm) tail, make a six-bead ladder (see "Flat herringbone basics"). Weave back to the start, so the working thread and the tail exit opposite sides of the first bead.

❸ Begin working in herringbone stitch (see "Flat herringbone basics"), with size 8ᵒs as the main beads and 11ᵒs as the edge beads. Stitch the number of rows determined by step 1.

❹ Following the pattern below, stitch the center portion of the bracelet by substituting a 4mm crystal for a size 8ᵒ bead where indicated.

❺ After completing the crystal section, stitch the number of rows determined by step 1 using 8ᵒs.

MAKE THE CLASP

❶ For the loop, bring the needle out the third bead in the last row. Make a loop of 11ᵒs long enough to accommodate the clasp bead. Go back through the first 11ᵒ strung and then go down the fourth bead in the last row to complete the loop (photo a). Weave back to the third bead in the last row and go through the loop again to reinforce it. Weave the tail into the beadwork, using a few half-hitch knots to secure it (see "Flat herringbone basics" and "Thread and knots," p. 4), and trim the tail close to the work.

❷ Weave the 10-in. starting tail through three or four rows from the starting edge, and exit a bead in one of the two middle stacks. String one size 11ᵒ seed bead, the clasp bead, and an 11ᵒ. Go back through the clasp bead and the first 11ᵒ (photo b). Sew back into the base on the other middle stack and pull it snug (photo c). Repeat the thread path to reinforce the clasp bead. Tie off the tail with half-hitch knots and trim.

Designed by Julia Gerlach.

MATERIALS

7½-in. (19cm) bracelet
- 48 4mm crystals
  24 color A
  24 color B
- 10g size 8ᵒ seed beads
- 2g size 11ᵒ seed beads
- Fireline fishing line, 6 lb. test
- beading needles, #12
- flat glass bead or rondelle for clasp

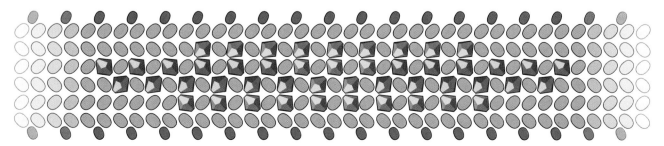

Asymmetrical lariat

Accent a long, supple rope stitched in herringbone with three or four strands of complementary beads to make a lariat. Begin by weaving a strip of four-bead-wide herringbone. Then string the beaded strands, passing each through a shank button, and ending each with a long fringe. Finally, make a loop at the other end.

STITCH THE LARIAT

❶ Thread a needle with a 60-in. (1.5m) length of conditioned Nymo. Leaving an 18-in. (46cm) tail, make a four-bead ladder (see "Flat herringbone basics," p. 6 and **figure 1**), alternating between light and dark beads (light, dark, light, dark). Zigzag back through the ladder for stability.

❷ Exiting the top of the ladder, begin herringbone stitch (see "Flat herringbone basics") by picking up a light bead and a dark bead. Go down through the second bead on the ladder (**figure 2**) and up through the third bead. Pick up a light and a dark again and go down through the fourth bead on the ladder.

❸ To turn the corner, pick up a dark bead and go back up through the last bead added on the second row (**figure 3**). Pick up a dark and a light bead and go down the second bead in the previous row. Come up through the third bead, pick up a dark and a light bead, and go down through the fourth bead on the row below. Pick up a light bead, turn the corner as before, and come back up through the last bead added in the third row.

❹ Continue working in herringbone stitch to the desired length (here, 20 in./51cm), picking up beads to match the color pattern established. If desired, substitute a few rows of bugle beads for some of the rows of seed beads. To make the turn at the end of a row of bugle beads, go down through the bugle below, pick up enough seed beads to cover the thread (it will depend on the length of the bugle bead), and go up through the last bugle added (**photo a**).

BEGINNING AND ENDING THREADS

Stop stitching when 4-6 in. (10-15cm) of thread remains. Leave the old thread as a marker for which bead the new thread should exit. See "Adding and ending thread," p. 6.

STRING THE STRANDS AND FRINGE

❶ Center a needle on a 60-in. length of Nymo. Working with doubled thread, enter the beadwork a few rows from the end and anchor the thread with a half-hitch knot (see "Thread and knots," p. 4). Weave the thread into the beadwork, as in "Adding and ending thread." Starting with an 8º, string about 7 in. (18cm) of larger beads interspersed with seed beads. Then string a 6º or 4mm bead, the shank button, and another 6º or 4mm bead. Continue the strand for another 3-5 in. (7.6-13cm) for the fringe, ending with a seed bead (**photo b**). Skip the last bead, go back up through the strand (**photo c**), and into the edge bead at the start of the fringe. Go down through the next bead along the edge (**photo d**).

❷ Make two or three more strands like the first, but go through the same 6º or

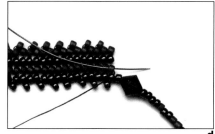

figure 1

figure 2

figure 3

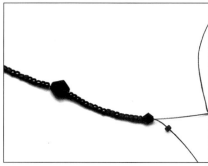

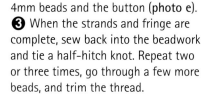

4mm beads and the button (**photo e**).

3 When the strands and fringe are complete, sew back into the beadwork and tie a half-hitch knot. Repeat two or three times, go through a few more beads, and trim the thread.

MAKE THE BUTTONHOLE

1 Thread a needle onto the lariat's 18-in. tail. Pick up two beads and go through the next bead. Instead of coming up the first bead in the next stitch, turn and sew back into the last bead added.

2 Make another stitch and turn as usual with an edge bead.

3 Repeat steps 1–2 until the first half of the loop is the desired length.

4 Sew back through the inner stack of beads to the base of the buttonhole and repeat steps 1–2 on the other side (**photo f**). Sew the two ends together (**photo g**). Repeat the thread path twice for stability, then weave through a few beads and make a half-hitch knot. Go through a few more beads, make another knot, go through

a few more beads, and trim the excess thread.

Designed by Cathy Collison, owner of Glass Garden Beads. Contact her by mail at 413 Division St. South, Northfield, MN 55057; by phone at (507) 645-0301; or by e-mail at ggarden@clearlakes.com. Visit the store website, glassgardenbeads.com.

Endless herringbone cuff

Combining beads in different shapes and finishes creates a deceptively complicated look in this flat herringbone cuff. But it's easy to stitch and works up quickly.

MAKING THE BASE

❶ Thread a needle with 3 yd. (2.7m) of Fireline. Make a ladder (see "Flat herringbone basics," p. 6 and **figures 1–3**), alternating a square and a triangle bead twice (four beads). Leave a 6-in. (15cm) tail.

❷ Pick up a square and a triangle. Go down through the second bead and up through the third in the ladder (**figure 4**).

❸ Pick up a square and a triangle. Go down through the fourth bead (a

MATERIALS

- 10g Japanese cube beads, 4mm
- 10g Japanese triangle beads, size 5º
- 10g Japanese seed beads, size 11º
- Fireline fishing line, 6-lb. test
- beading needles, #10

square) in the ladder (**figure 5**).

❹ String two size 11º seed beads to turn the corner and go up through the last triangle in the new row (**figure 6**).

❺ Repeat from step 2 until the bracelet fits around the widest part of your hand.

JOINING THE ENDS

❶ Connect the ends by weaving the tail from the end of the bracelet into the first few rows of the beginning of the bracelet. Then weave the tail from the beginning into the last few rows of the end. Make sure the alternating triangle/square pattern matches up.

❷ The square at the edge of the last row will not have two size 11º seed beads next to it. Add these beads as you weave the ends together (**figure 7**). Weave in the tails and tie off, using half-hitch knots (see "Thread and knots," p. 4). Trim the tails.

FILLING IN THE GAPS

❶ Thread a needle with 3 yd. of Fireline and come up through any edge square.

❷ Pick up one size 11º bead (**figure 8, a**) and go down through the next triangle in the same row.

❸ Pick up one size 11º and go up through the next square in the same row.

❹ Pick up one size 11º bead and go down through the last triangle in the same row. Now pass the needle down the two size 11º beads on the edge and up through the square on the next row below (**figure 8, b**).

❺ Repeat steps 2-4 (**b–c**) until all the spaces are filled. Weave the thread in and tie off as above. Then trim the tails.

Designed by Anna Nehs. Visit her website, beadivine.biz, to see more of her work, or e-mail her at beadbiz@hotmail.com.

figure 1

figure 2

figure 3

figure 4

figure 5

figure 6

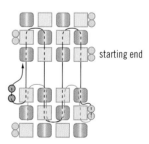

starting end

figure 7

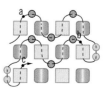

figure 8

Blooming bracelet

You don't need a green thumb to make this flowery bracelet. Simply build a base using chunky beads and layer it with clinging vines and budding blooms. The turn from one row to the next on the base is a slight variation from that taught in other projects in this book. The turn eliminates the need for edge beads, but it also forces the beads along both edges to line up parallel instead of tilting toward each other. However, since the real focus of this bracelet is the embellishment, the atypical formation isn't very noticeable. The stitched base goes together easily, so you get to the embellishment quickly.

Use Power Pro or other braided thread for everything except the embellishment. For this section, work with conditioned Nymo (see "Thread

and knots," p. 4). If desired, add picot edging to one or both ends by picking up three seed beads and securing them between two base beads.

MAKE THE BASE

❶ With 2 yd. (1.8m) of Power Pro, stitch a ten-bead ladder (see "Flat herringbone basics," p. 6 and **figure 1**) using 8º or 3.3mm seed beads. Weave the tail into the beadwork, tying a few half-hitch knots (see "Thread and knots") as you go.

❷ To start a row of herringbone, exit the first ladder bead. String two 8ºs or 3.3s and go through the second ladder bead (**figure 2, a–b**). Come back up the third ladder bead. Continue stitching across the row. To make the turn, go down through the second-to-last ladder

bead and come back up through the last ladder bead (**figure 2, c–d**).

❸ Repeat step 2 until the bracelet is the desired length (this one is 55 rows). When the working thread is 6 in. (15cm) long, tie it off within the beadwork and add a new one (see "Flat herringbone basics").

ATTACH TWO BUTTONS

Weave through the beads and exit the third bead in the third row. String three 11ºs, a button, and three 11ºs (**figure 3**). Go back through the base bead again. Reinforce the section by passing through the beads two more times. Repeat to add a second button, starting at the eighth bead in the third row. Weave in the thread as in step 1.

MATERIALS

7-in. (18cm) bracelet

- Japanese seed beads
  20g size 8º or 3.3mm, green
  6g size 11º, green
  1g size 11º, pink
- 50–60 8 x 5mm leaf beads
  (msmaddiesbeads@nyc.rr.com)
- 50–60 5mm Czech glass flower rondelles
- 50–60 4mm round beads
- 2 ⅜-in. (10mm) shank buttons
- beading needles, #10
- Power Pro, 20 lb. test, moss green
- Nymo D, conditioned with
  Thread Heaven

ADD EMBELLISHMENTS

With 2 yd. of conditioned Nymo, weave through the herringbone base, coming out where you want to anchor the first vine. String six green 11ºs, a leaf, a rondelle, a 4mm bead, and a pink 11º. Skip the end bead and go through the 4mm, rondelle, and leaf (**figure 4**). Secure the vine by sewing through a nearby base bead so the green 11ºs lie flat. Sew through two or three base beads and make another flowering vine. Continue, covering the base as desired.

FINISH WITH LOOPS

Secure 2 ft. (61cm) of Power Pro in the ladder beads. Come out the second bead from the end. Pick up 23 green 11ºs, or enough to fit around the button. Go through the bead next to the anchor bead (**figure 5**), then retrace the thread path twice. Repeat to make a second loop, two beads from the other end.

Designed by Merle Berelowitz. Contact her at msmaddiesbeads@nyc.rr.com or at 415 E. 37th St., Apt. 36C, New York, NY 10016.

figure 1

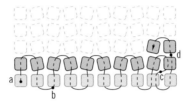

figure 2

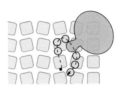

figure 3

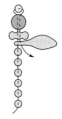

figure 4

figure 5

Scalloped bracelet

Inspired by a chain taught by Margo Field at a *Bead&Button* show a couple of years ago, this fun bracelet uses increases and decreases to achieve its scalloped shape.

The bracelet is stitched with doubled thread to help maintain firm tension. After stitching each row, pull to keep the thread tension taut. If the beads do not sit in cupped pairs, coax them into place to form the herringbone pattern. Use slightly smaller contrast-color beads on your increase and decrease rows to keep the bracelet from bulging.

BRACELET BASE

❶ Center a needle on 10 ft. (3m) of Silamide. Make a four-bead ladder (see "Flat herringbone basics," p. 6).

❷ Zigzag back to the row's first bead (**figure 1**).

❸ Pick up two MC beads and sew through the second bead on the ladder. Sew up through the third bead. Pick up two MC beads and sew through the last bead (**figure 2**).

❹ Pick up one contrast color (CC) bead and sew through the last MC bead added (**figure 3**).

❺ Repeat steps 3–4 until the strip is about 2-2½ in. (5–6.3cm) long or about one-third of your wrist's circumference.

SCALLOP INSETS

❶ To start the first increase row, pick up two MC beads and sew through the second bead in the previous row. Pick up one CC bead and sew up through the third MC bead in the previous row. Pick up two MC beads and sew through the last bead in the row (**figure 4**).

❷ Pick up one CC bead and sew through the last MC bead added.

❸ For the next row, repeat step 1, inserting two CC beads in the middle instead of one (**figure 5**). Repeat step 2.

❹ Pick up two MC beads and sew through the second MC bead and the next CC bead added in the previous row. Pick up two CC beads and sew through the second CC bead and the next MC bead in the row. Pick up two MC beads and and sew through the last MC bead in the row. Repeat step 2 (**figure 6**).

❺ Repeat step 4 three times.

❻ To sew the first decrease row, pick up two MC beads and sew through the second MC bead in the previous row.

Sew through the two CC beads and the next MC bead in the row. Pick up two MC beads and sew through the last MC bead in the row. Repeat step 2 (**figure 7**).

❼ Repeat step 1 to insert one CC bead between the two pairs of MC beads added for the next row. Repeat step 2 (**figure 8**).

❽ Work four rows of herringbone without the scallop.

❾ Repeat steps 1–7 to add a second scallop to the bracelet.

❿ Repeat steps 8–9 to add a third scallop to the bracelet.

COMPLETING THE BRACELET

❶ Work in herringbone until the bracelet encircles your wrist with a ½-in. (1.3cm) overlap. After adding the last row of herringbone, sew back through the two previous rows, repeating the thread path and keeping the tension taut.

❷ Sew one side of the snap fastener to this end of the bracelet. Finish the thread with a few half-hitch knots (see "Thread and knots," p. 4) and glue the knots. When the glue is dry, trim the thread.

❸ Thread a needle on the tails at the other end of the bracelet. Sew the second half of the snap to the other side of the bracelet and finish the thread as in step 2.

Designed by Jane Tyson of Hobart, Tasmania, in Australia. Contact her at lj_tyson@aapt.net.au.

> ### MATERIALS
> - 20g 8º seed beads, main color
> - 10g 8º seed beads, contrast color
> - ⅜-in. (6mm) snap fastener
> - Silamide or other thick, strong thread
> - beading needles, #10

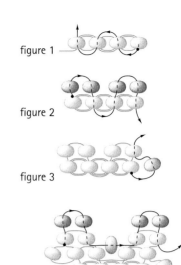

figure 1

figure 2

figure 3

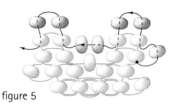

figure 4

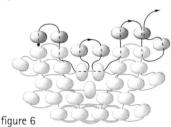

figure 5

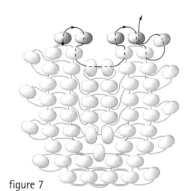

figure 6

figure 7

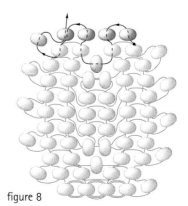

figure 8

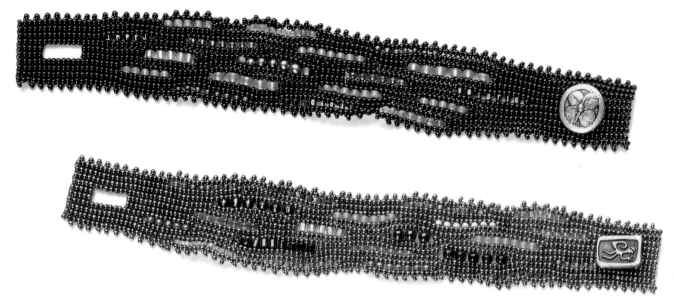

Inset bracelet

Inserting short lengths of contrasting beads in a basic herringbone design produces an interesting and complex-looking texture.

❶ Thread a needle with a 60-in. (1.5m) length of conditioned Nymo. Make a ten-bead ladder (see "Flat herringbone basics," p. 6 and **figure 1**) with your main-color size 11º beads. Zigzag back through the ladder for stability.

❷ Make five rows in herringbone stitch (see "Flat herringbone basics") using just the main color 11ºs.

❸ To begin the buttonhole, *make two herringbone stitches. Instead of coming up through the first bead of the next stitch, go back up through the last bead just added (**photo a** and **figure 2**), turning without adding the edge bead. Working in the other direction, make two more stitches, and this time include the edge bead on the turn.* Repeat from * to * until the buttonhole is the desired length and the last row ends at the inner edge (**figure 3, point a**).

❹ Sew down through the inner stack of beads to the bottom edge of the buttonhole (**figure 3, a–b**). Follow the existing thread path to weave over the middle stack and exit the first bead of the next stitch (**figure 3, b–c**).

❺ Begin stitching herringbone rows as you did on the first side of the buttonhole (**figure 3 c–d**), making the same number of rows.

❻ To close the buttonhole, pick up two 11ºs and sew down through the top two beads in the last row (**figure 4, a–b**). Go back up through the two beads just added (**photo b**), pick up two more, go through the same two beads again, and go back down through the two beads just added (**figure 4, b–c**). Sew up through the top two beads on the other side of the buttonhole, go down through the last two added, and back up through the two that were just gone through (**photo c** and **figure 4, c–d**). Weave to the edge and resume basic herringbone stitch.

❼ Stitch one or two more rows of herringbone across the top of the completed buttonhole.

❽ Once you're past the buttonhole, you can begin inserting other colors and sizes of beads into the bracelet. Continue stitching in flat herringbone, but add insert beads as follows:

Pick up a main color 11º, an accent bead, and the second main color 11º and sew into the next bead (**photo d** and **figure 5**). Complete the row with main color 11ºs.

When adding most inset beads, depending on their size, add the bead in one row. Go through it in the next (**photo e**) and possibly the next row before inserting another bead.

To ease the transition back to basic herringbone at the end of an inset section, use a main color 11º in place of an inset bead. This creates a smaller gap that needs to be covered.

❾ Continue stitching the bracelet in herringbone, adding insets as desired, until it is within an inch of the finished length. Stitch another few rows with main-color 11ºs only and check the fit.

❿ When you reach the place where the button should go, add a shank button like an insert bead. If using a button without a shank, sew it on when the bracelet is finished. Whichever type of button you use, be sure to reinforce the join by repeating the thread path several times.

⓫ Sew another five or six rows after adding the button. When complete, sew into the beadwork, tie a half-hitch knot, go through a few more more beads, tie another knot, go through a few more beads, and trim.

Designed by Lori Schmidt and Cathy Collison. Cathy owns Glass Garden Beads. Visit the store website, glassgardenbeads.com. Contact her by mail at 413 Division St. South, Northfield, MN 55057; by phone at (507) 645-0301; or by e-mail at ggarden@clearlakes.com.

a

b

c

d

e

figure 1

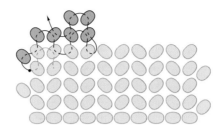

figure 2

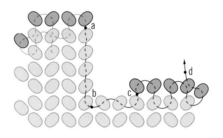

figure 3

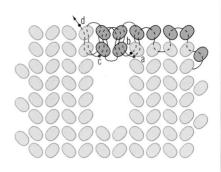

figure 4

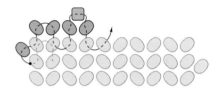

figure 5

MATERIALS

7½-in. (19cm) bracelet:

- 20g 11º seed beads or Japanese cylinder beads
- 1–2g each of a variety of seed, triangle, or hex beads in assorted colors and sizes from 15º to 6º
- button
- Nymo B beading thread or Silamide, size A
- beading needles, #12 or 13
- beeswax or Thread Heaven for Nymo

Rainbow collar

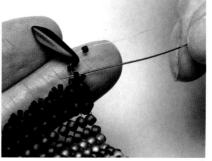

Use the traditional herringbone start on this stunning collar. It's a little tricky to understand at first, but stick with it and you'll master it in no time.

The keys to making a collar with a gentle curve that lies gracefully across your shoulders are a very gradual increase in bead sizes and careful tension. Czech 6°s and Japanese 8°s and 11°s are essential if the collar is to curve correctly. You also need to keep the tension consistently firm with very little thread showing between beads.

When you need to add thread, first check to see if there are any mistakes that need to be fixed. Leave the needle on about 6 in. (15cm) of old thread and start another needle with 2-2½ yd.

MATERIALS
- 6g Japanese seed beads, size 11° (no substitutions)
- 15g each Japanese seed beads, size 8°, four colors (no substitutions)
- 30g Czech seed beads, size 6° (no substitutions)
- 10g Japanese cylinder beads (Delicas)
- **52 drop beads or other accent beads**
- small button for clasp
- beading needles, #10 or 12
- Nymo D beading thread or Silamide

(1.8-2.3m) of thread. Working 6 in. (15cm) from the end, tie the new thread around the old one and slide the knot against the beadwork. Tie the two short

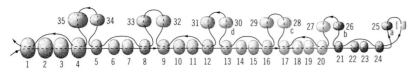

figure 1

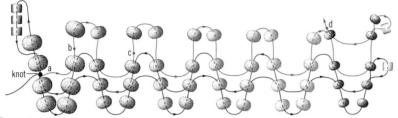

figure 2

tails together with a surgeon's knot (see "Thread and knots," p. 4) and hide the knot inside the closest bead.

Work the ends into the necklace by going back through just one row and making three half-hitch knots (see "Thread and knots") about 1¼-in. (3.2cm) apart. Don't pull too tightly—you don't want the beads to pucker or the join to show.

COLLAR

Unlike most necklaces, this collar is stitched across its width, not from end-to-end. I tell my students they need to think sideways to prepare themselves for this project.

1 String a stop bead near the tail end of a 2-yd. length of thread and tie it in place (you'll remove it later). The herringbone weave is worked in multiples of four, so pick up four 6ºs, four 8ºs of each color, and four 11ºs (24 beads total). Since not all 8ºs are exactly the same size, you may have to rearrange the colors so your beads are graduated from largest to smallest.

2 Pick up one 11º and one cylinder bead. Turn and sew back through bead 24 and bead 21 (figure 1, a–b). Skip two beads between stitches. Be careful not to pierce any threads.

3 Pick up an 11º and an 8º. Here's the rule for determining which beads and colors to use: The first bead you pick up should match the one your thread is exiting; the second should match the bead you're about to enter. Sew through beads 20 and 17 (figure 1, b–c).

4 Pick up two 8ºs. Sew into beads

16 and 13 (figure 1, c–d). Continue across the row.

5 Remove the stop bead. Tighten the tail and needle ends of the thread until the beads form a pattern of six Vs (photo a, p.19). Use your thumbnail to coax the beads into position. Each stack except the last one will have three beads.

6 Pick up two 6ºs and three cylinders, slide them against the beadwork, and hold them in place. Skip the cylinders and the adjoining 6º and sew through the next 6º. Tie the thread's tail and needle ends together. Sew through the top 6º bead in the next V (figure 2, a–b).

7 Pick up a 6º and an 8º, matching colors as in step 3. Sew down through the top of the next bead (an 8º) and up through the bead after that (figure 2, b–c).

8 Stitch across the row. Pick up two beads each time and only sew through the top beads in each stack. Pick up two 11ºs and one cylinder. Skip the cylinder and the second 11º. Sew down through the first 11º and up through the 11º at the top of the next stack (figure 2, c–d). Hold the beads in place as you make the turn at each edge so they stay in the right position when you stitch. Make sure the beads are lined up correctly before you continue.

9 At the end of this row, pick up two 6ºs and three cylinders as in step 6. Skip the cylinders and the adjoining 6º and sew through the next 6º to make the turn.

10 After completing the first few rows, you'll begin to see the herringbone

pattern. You'll also notice that the necklace is starting to curve. That's the effect you're after. Keep the tension consistently firm as you stitch and continue until your necklace fits comfortably around your neck.

DROPS

1 Start with a 2-yd. length of thread. Secure the thread in the edge row of 6ºs with at least three half-hitch knots spaced 1½ in. (3.8cm) apart. Exit through a 6º at the corner along the bottom edge.

2 Sew through two of the closest three cylinders (photo b, p.19). Pick up a drop bead (if using a side-drilled drop, add a cylinder on either side to hide the thread) and sew back into the middle cylinder from the opposite side. Your thread will encircle the middle bead (photo c, p.19).

3 Sew through the next cylinder, three 6ºs, and two cylinders. Add the next drop bead. Continue across the bottom edge.

CLOSURE

1 Secure about 2 ft. (60cm) of thread in the second (counting from the inner edge) row of 11ºs with several half-hitch knots and exit the edge bead of that row.

2 Pick up eight to ten 11ºs, string the button, and pick up an equal number of 11ºs. Sew into a few beads on the next row of 8ºs (photo d, p.19). Reverse direction and sew back through the 11º row to the edge.

3 Sew through the newly added beads and into the beadwork at least four times to reinforce the closure.

4 To make the loop portion of the closure, repeat the steps on the other end of the necklace, excluding the button, and stringing enough seed beads to fit over the button.

Designed by Carole Horn, a renowned instructor from New York. Reach her at (212) 650-1778.

TUBULAR HERRINGBONE

Tubular herringbone basics

TUBULAR HERRINGBONE

To work tubular herringbone, make a ladder of the desired number of beads (an even number, in this case four) and join it into a ring. String two beads and go down the next bead on the first row (the ladder). Come up the next bead and repeat. There will be two stitches when you've gone down the fourth bead

(**a–b** in the figure at right).

You need to work a "step up" to be in position to start the next row. To do this, come up the bead next to the one your needle is exiting and the first bead of the first stitch (**c–d**).

Continue adding two beads per stitch and stepping up at the end of each round.

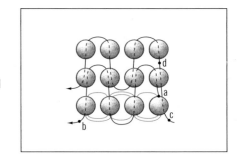

CRIMPING

1 Position the crimp bead in the notch closest to the crimping pliers' handle.
2 Separate the wires and firmly squeeze the crimp.
3 Move the crimp into the notch at the pliers' tip and hold the crimp as shown. Squeeze the crimp bead, folding it in half at the indentation.
4 Test that the folded crimp is secure.

WRAPPED LOOPS

1 Make sure you have at least 1¼ in. (3.2cm) of wire above the bead. With the tip of your chainnose pliers, grasp the wire directly above the bead. Bend the wire (above the pliers) into a right angle.
2 Using roundnose pliers, position the jaws in the bend.

3 Bring the wire over the top jaw of the roundnose pliers.
4 Reposition the pliers' lower jaw snugly into the loop. Curve the wire downward around the bottom of the roundnose pliers. This is the first half of a wrapped loop.
5 Position the chainnose pliers' jaws across the loop.
6 Wrap the wire around the wire stem, covering the stem between the loop

and the top of the bead. Trim the excess wire and press the cut end close to the wraps with chainnose pliers.

Rope necklace

MATERIALS
necklace 27 in. (69cm)
- 2-in. (5cm) diameter stone donut (shown in dalmatian jasper)
- 16 14 x 20mm stone pebble beads (shown in dalmatian jasper)
- seed beads, size 11º
  15g main color (off-white)
  10g accent color A (black)
  5g accent color B (cocoa)
- Nymo B
- beading needles, #12

Stone donuts, also known as pi, come in a great variety of sizes and colors at reasonable prices, and they make wonderful focal beads. This necklace combines the distinctively spotted stone known as dalmatian jasper with matte-finish seed beads. The result is a tailored necklace with classic appeal. For a more colorful piece, try this necklace with a suitably vibrant focal bead; you can easily adapt this design to your personal color palette.

INNER ROPE
❶ Using a 60-in. (1.5m) length of Nymo, stitch a four-bead ladder (see "Tubular herringbone basics," p. 22) with accent color A beads. Leave a 12-in. (31cm) tail. Join the first bead to the last to form a ring (**figure 1,** p. 24). This becomes round 1 of the rope.
❷ Continue in tubular herringbone, stitching a four-bead rope as follows (**figure 2**). Make sure to step up between rounds.
Rounds 2–3: accent color B
Round 4: A

Rounds 5–13: main color (MC)
Round 14: A
Rounds 15–16: B
Round: 17: A
❸ Pick up a stone pebble and two As and slide them against the last row. Go back through the pebble and one bead in round 17. Tighten the thread. Come up through a neighboring bead on round 17 (**photo a**) and go back through the pebble.
❹ Pick up two As and go through the pebble as before. Go down and up through the two remaining beads in

a

b

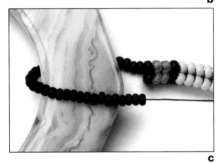

c

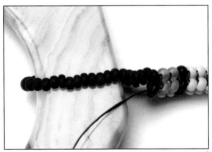

d

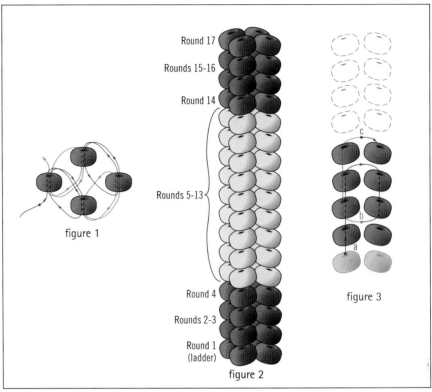

figure 1

figure 2

figure 3

round 17. Go back through the pebble and one of the newly added beads. Tighten the thread (**photo b**). (The four seed beads added in steps 3 and 4 become round 1 of the next herringbone sequence.)

⑤ Continue stitching the four-bead herringbone rope as follows:
Rounds 19–34: Repeat rounds 2–17.
Rounds 35–47: Repeat rounds 5–17.

⑥ Repeat steps 3–5 until you've strung four pebbles, ending with a round of As. Repeat rounds 2–17 to finish the last pattern repeat.

⑦ Stitch the next 5–6 in. (13–15cm) using As. (This is the solid black section

at the back of the necklace.)

⑧ Stitch the second half of the strap to mirror the first. End the thread, leaving a 12-in. (31cm) tail.

OUTER ROPE

① Stitch a four-bead ladder using As. Join the first bead to the last to form a ring.

② Work the next two rounds using Bs, then work a round using As.

③ String a pebble and add a round of As as in steps 3–4 above.

④ Repeat rounds 2–17 followed by rounds 5–17, adding pebbles until you've strung four pebbles. Then repeat rounds 2–17 one more time.

⑤ Stitch the back of the necklace using As as in step 7, making it 1–2 in. (2.5–5cm) longer than the back section of the inner rope.

⑥ Stitch the second half of the strap to mirror the first.

FOCAL BEAD

① Thread a needle on the tail at either end of the inner rope and exit an A bead. Pick up as many As as you need to encircle the donut's edge (**photo c**).

② Go through another A bead on the end of the rope to connect the loop.

Turn and exit a neighboring A bead on the rope (**photo d**).

③ Repeat steps 1–2 to connect a second loop to the rope. (String an equal number of beads on each loop.) Exit an A bead with your needle pointing toward the loops.

④ To weave the loops together, go through the first three beads on the loop closest to the needle. Turn and go through the third and second bead on the other loop (**figure 3, a–b**).

⑤ Go through the second through fourth beads on the first loop. Turn and go back through the fourth and third beads on the other loop (**b–c**). Repeat until the loops are connected. Secure the thread and trim the tail.

⑥ Attach the other end of the inner rope and the ends of the outer rope in the same way. Make sure the ends of the outer rope are outside the inner rope.

⑦ Stitch the two straps together at the back of the neck, if desired.

Designed by Lisa Olson Tune. Contact her at tunebdbdbd@aol.com.

Roller bead bracelet

MATERIALS

Makes a pair of beads

- 18 4mm Swarovski crystals
- 1g seed beads, size 8º
- 2g Japanese cylinder or seed beads, size 11º
- 1g triangle beads, size 11º
- Silamide or Power Pro
- beading needles, #12

Work a tube of herringbone with multiple bead shapes and sizes for easy beaded beads that nestle together when strung to make a bracelet. You can make these beads with any bead shape, just make sure the bead sizes graduate to form the "bump."

❶ Working with a 5-ft. (1.5m) length of doubled thread, string two triangle beads to 8 in. (20cm) from the end.

❷ Sew up through the first bead and down through the second bead (**figure 1**, p.26).

❸ Pick up a triangle, sew down through the second bead and up through the bead just added. Keep the thread's tension tight and make sure the beads are side by side (**figure 2, a–b**).

❹ Continue working the ladder for a total of six beads (**figure 2, b–c** and "Flat herringbone basics," p. 6).

❺ Sew the first and last beads of the

a

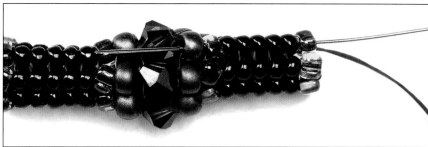

c

b

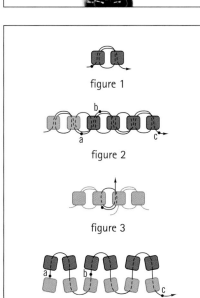

figure 1

figure 2

figure 3

figure 4

figure 5

bead 1 (bump-in-the-middle)
Row 1: size 11º triangles
Rows 2-6: 11ºs
Row 7: size 11º triangles
Row 8: 8ºs
Row 9: 4mm crystals
Row 10: 8ºs
Row 11: size 11º triangles
Rows 12-16: 11ºs
Row 17: size 11º triangles

bead 2 (dumbell)
Row 1: 11ºs
Row 2: size 11º triangles
Row 3: 8ºs
Row 4: 4mm crystals
Row 5: 8ºs
Row 6: size 11º triangles
Rows 7-11: 11ºs
Row 12: size 11º triangles
Row 13: 8ºs
Row 14: 4mm crystals
Row 15: 8ºs
Row 16: size 11º triangles
Row 17: 11ºs

ladder together to form a ring
(**figure 3**).

6 Refer to the chart above for bead 1
and work rows 2-17 in herringbone. To
start row 2, pick up two 11ºs, sew down
through the next bead on the ladder,
and up through the third (**figure 4,
a-b**). Repeat around the ring (**b-c**).

7 After you add the last pair on the
row, step up through the row's first
bead so you are in position to start
the next row (**figure 5, a-b**). On row 3,
the bead pairs added will form a V
(**photo a**).

8 When you add the crystals in row 9,
use the needle to position the crystals
so they stack pointing up (**photo b**).

9 Sew through each stacked column
of beads to stiffen the roller bead
(**photo c**).

10 Secure the thread ends with a few
half-hitch knots (see "Thread and
knots," p. 4) between beads and trim.

11 Repeat steps 1–10 and refer to the
chart for bead 2 to make the dumbbell shaped roller bead.

EDITOR'S NOTE:
*As you work herringbone stitch, make
sure each new pair of beads sits side by
side and stacks on the previous row. Pull
the thread tight to lock the stitch
in place before adding the next pair
of beads.*

BRACELET MATERIALS

- roller beads
- 50 or more 4-6mm round beads or rondelles
- 4-5 ft. (1.2-1.5m) 20- or 22 gauge wire
- flexible beading wire
- 4 crimp beads
- two-strand clasp
- chainnose and roundnose pliers
- crimping pliers (optional)

MAKE THE BRACELET

❶ Cut 3 in. (7.6cm) of wire and make a wrapped loop (see p. 22) at one end. String a silver spacer bead, a roller bead, and another silver spacer. Make another wrapped loop at the wire's opposite end. Prepare enough roller-bead components to encircle your wrist. Allow about 1 in. (2.5cm) for the clasp.

❷ Cut two 12-in. (31cm) lengths of flexible beading wire. String each wire through a crimp bead and a loop on a two-hole clasp. Take each wire back through its crimp bead, tighten the wires, and crimp the crimps (see p. 22).

❸ String two 4-6mm round beads and a cylinder bead on each wire, hiding the tails. String one wire through each loop at the ends of a bump-in-the-middle component. String a cylinder, a round, and a cylinder on each wire.

❹ String the wires through the loops on a dumbbell component. The roller beads should nestle together. String a cylinder, a round bead, and a cylinder on each wire. Continue stringing the bracelet, alternating the types of roller beads and spacing them with cylinder-round-cylinder combinations.

❺ When you have reached the desired length, string two round beads and a crimp on each wire. Check the fit and adjust accordingly. Slide each wire through a loop on the other half of the

Rainbow bracelet color chart

Make the desired number of beads using the BEAD 1 and BEAD 2 color combinations listed below. The color codes listed are for Delica brand Japanese cylinder beads.

° Red DB774 & DB43 & 18 red crystals
° Pink DB874 & DB1335 & 18 pink crystals
° Purple DB783 & DB610 & 18 light amethyst crystals
° Blue DB696 & DB240 & 18 sapphire crystals
° Turquoise DB793 & DB608 & 18 turquoise crystals
° Green DB767 & DB713 & 18 emerald green crystals
° Lime green DB763 & DB274 & 18 peridot crystals
° Yellow DB751 & DB1301 & 18 jonquil crystals
° Orange DB682 & DB855 & 18 Indian red crystals
° Gold DB1333 & DB781 & 18 topaz crystals
° Brown DB709 & DB764 & 18 dark topaz crystals
° Gray DB247 & DB761 & 18 black diamond crystals
° Peach DB206 & DB70 & 18 peach crystals
° Fuchsia DB1310 & DB1340 & 18 fuchsia crystals
° Olive DB182 & DB311 & 18 olivine crystals
° Cream DB204 & DB352 & 18 light Colorado crystals
° White DB202 & DB357 & 18 white opal crystals

clasp and back through the crimp and a few beads. Crimp the crimps and trim the wire tails.

Designed by Dona Anderson, author of two bead pattern books, who teaches throughout the United States. See more of her work at beadingheartdesigns.org; e-mail her at beadheart@aol.com.

Honeysuckle earrings

Attract attention with these pretty herringbone flower earrings. They're easy to make and stitch up quickly.

BULB

❶ Pick up a size 8º seed bead and slide it to the end of 1 yd. (90cm) of thread, leaving a 4-in. (10cm) tail. Secure the bead with a surgeon's knot (see "Thread and knots," p. 4). Pick up a 6mm bead and four 11ºs in color A. Sew back through the first 11º to form a picot, then continue through the 6mm bead and the 8º (**figure 1, a–b**). Sew back through the 6mm bead.

❷ Make two more picots as in step 1 (**photo a**).

❸ Exit the 8º and tie the tails together in a square knot (see "Thread and knots"). Put a dot of glue on the knot, let dry, then trim the tails.

TUBE

❶ On 2 yd. (1.8m) of thread, stitch a two-bead ladder, eight stacks long in color B (see "Flat herringbone basics," p. 6 and **photo b**), leaving a 12-in. (30cm) tail.

❷ Connect the first beads of the ladder to the last by sewing through

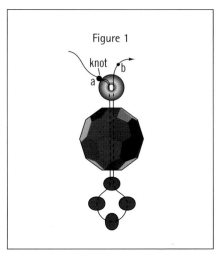

Figure 1

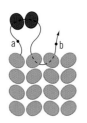

Figure 2

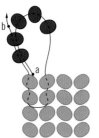

Figure 3

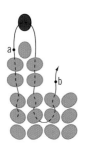

Figure 4

a

b

c

d

e

MATERIALS

earrings, one pair

- Japanese seed beads, size 11º
  1g color A
  5g color B
  1g color C
- 2 Japanese seed beads, size 8º, color A
- 2 6–8mm round beads (hole large enough for several thread passes)
- 2 bead caps or small flower beads
- earring findings
- Nymo B
- beading needles, #12
- G-S Hypo Cement

the first stack, the last stack, and the first stack again. The tail and working thread will exit on opposite sides of the ladder (**photo c**).

❸ Work in tubular herringbone from the top row of the ladder (see "Tubular herringbone basics," p. 22 and **figure 2, a–b**). Continue in tubular herringbone for a total of 12 rows, stepping up after each row. (For a shorter earring, reduce the number of herringbone rows.)

PETALS

❶ Position your thread so it exits the first bead added in the last herringbone row (**figure 3, point a**).

❷ Pick up five Bs and sew down through two beads in the next stack. Sew up through two beads in the first stack and the first two beads of the five (**a–b**). Pick up a B and sew down through four beads in the second stack and up through two beads in the third stack (**figure 4, a–b**).

❸ Repeat, adding three more petals. Set the working thread aside.

TOP

❶ Thread a needle on the 12-in. tail and work two rows of tubular herringbone in C.

❷ For row 3, pick up only one C for each stitch. Then sew through the four beads just added and pull them together into a tight circle (**photo d**).

❸ Pick up the working thread and sew through one of the stacks of herringbone, exiting across from the thread tail. Pick up a bead cap and six Cs. Go back through the bead cap and tie the thread tails together with a square knot (see "Thread and knots"). Do not cut the threads.

ASSEMBLY

❶ Using the working thread, sew through the center of the flower tube. Pick up 15 Bs, sew through the 8º at the top of the bulb, and go back through the seed beads and the bead cap (**photo e**). Tighten the thread to pull the seed beads up into the tube. Don't pull too tightly or the tube may bend.

❷ Sew through the six-bead loop, and back through the bead cap. Tie the threads together with a square knot.

❸ Secure the tails in the beadwork, tying half-hitch knots (see "Thread and knots") between beads. Trim the tails.

❹ Open the earring finding's loop and attach it to the six-bead loop.

❺ Make a second earring to match the first.

Designed by Stephanie Eddy. Contact her at (208) 853-7988 or kitsforsale@stephanieeddy.com. To see more of her work, visit her website, stephanieeddy.com.

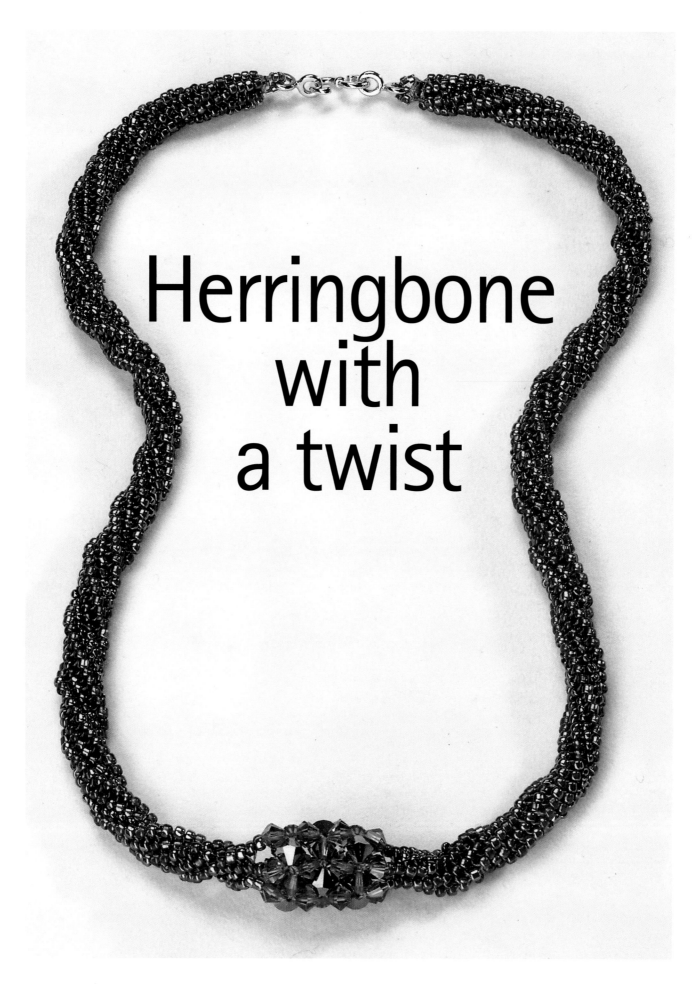

Herringbone
with
a twist

This choker looks and feels like ordinary herringbone. But when you look closer, you'll notice a subtle spiral in the pattern. That's because the thread path is a little different than that of standard herringbone. After adding each pair of beads, you go down two beads but come up only the top bead in the next stack. You don't follow the normal step up for tubular herringbone either.

The crystal centerpiece, which is stitched in the middle of the rope, adds a special touch.

FIRST SIDE

❶ To begin, thread a beading needle with 1½–2 yd. (1.4–1.8m) of Silamide or Nymo B. Make a ladder two beads tall and six rows long using 11º seed beads (see "Flat herringbone basics," p. 6 and **figure 1**). Leave a starting tail of at least 12 in. (31cm) for attaching the clasp.

❷ Join the ladder into a ring by going down the first pair of beads and then back up the last pair (**photo a**). Go back through the first stack again.

❸ To begin round 1, the needle should exit the ladder in the opposite direction from the thread tail. Pick up two size 11ºs. Pass the needle down both beads of the next stack and up only the top bead of the following stack (**photo b**). You'll see a little thread at the beginning of this round. Repeat once. For the third and last stitch, pick up an 11º, a 15º, and an 11º. Go down the top bead of the last stack (**photo c**).

❹ To begin round 2, come up only the top 11º of the next stack (**photo d**). Note: a normal step up would go up two beads. Pick up two 11ºs and go down the top two beads of the next stack. Come up only the top bead of the next stack to begin the next stitch (**photo e**). Remember, the thread path for both sides is UP ONE, DOWN TWO! Make a second stitch like the first. For the final stitch, come up the first 11º of the three-bead stitch on the previous round, pick up an 11º, a 15º, and an 11º, and go down the second 11º of the previous three-bead stitch (**photo f**).

❺ Repeat round 2 until your necklace is 8½ in. (22cm) long or half the desired length minus 2 in. (5cm) to allow for the clasp and crystal centerpiece. Note: Now that the spiral is established, you only go down one bead at a time before

a

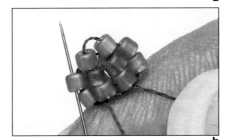

b

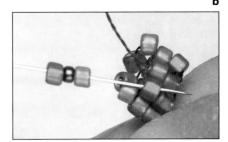

c

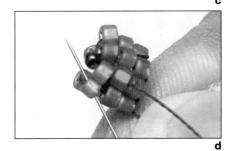

d

stepping up to the next row.

❻ To add thread, see **figure 2**. Thread a new needle. Starting four beads down in the stack before the one the old thread exits, pass the new needle up three beads. Then go down three in the stack before (**a–b**). Come back up the first three beads (**b–c**). Tie two or three half-hitch knots (see "Thread and knots," p. 4) between beads as you make this circle. Pass the needle up the top bead of the next stack where the old thread exits (**c–d**). Now end the old thread. Go down four of the next stack (**e–f**). Circle through two stacks as before, tying two half-hitch knots (**f–g**). Go through a few more beads before trimming the old thread.

❼ Work the last two rounds before the crystal centerpiece starting with a new 2-yd. thread. Work as you would normal herringbone—only come up one bead and go down one bead—and do not add the

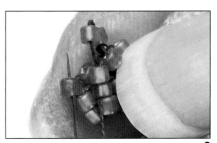

e

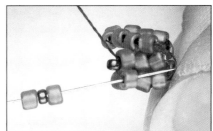

f

g

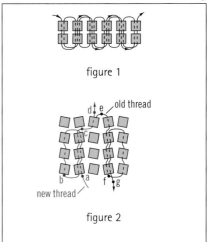

figure 1

figure 2

15º beads. Work a normal step up at the end of each round (see the first "Note" in step 4).

CRYSTAL CENTERPIECE

Round 1: Exit the first bead, pick up a 4mm crystal, a 5mm crystal, and a 4mm crystal. Go down the first bead of the next stack and come up the first bead of the next (**photo g**). The crystals will be wobbly, but don't worry. Repeat twice more to circle the tube. Follow the thread path again without adding beads. If the crystals are still wobbly, repeat.

Round 2: With the needle exiting a 5mm

bicone, pick up a 4mm crystal and go through the next 5mm (**photo h**). Pick up another 4mm and go through the third 5mm. Pick up a third 4mm and go through the first 5mm. Repeat the thread path. End exiting a 5mm.

Round 3: Pick up a 4mm, a 5mm, and a 4mm and go through the next 5mm of round 2 (**photo i**). Repeat twice, then secure with another thread pass.

Round 4: Repeat round 2.

Round 5: Repeat round 3.

Round 6: Repeat round 2.

Round 7: Exiting a 4mm crystal, pick up two 4mm crystals and go through the next 4mm on the previous round (**photo j**). Repeat around. Do not retrace the thread path as before.

SECOND SIDE

❶ Exiting a new 4mm crystal, pick up two 11ºs and go down the next new 4mm. Go through the next perpendicular 4mm and come back up the next new 4mm (**photo k**). Repeat. Pick up the last two 11ºs, go down the last new crystal, through the horizontal crystal and up the first 4mm and the 11º above it.

❷ On round 2, pick up two 11ºs and go down the next 11º and the crystal below it. Go through the horizontal crystal and come back up the next 4mm and the 11º above it (**photo l**). Repeat twice. End by exiting a 4mm and the two 11ºs above it.

❸ Round 3 begins the pattern of the second half of your choker. Pick up two 11ºs, go down one 11º on the next stack (the thread path for this row is UP ONE, DOWN ONE). Repeat. Come up the last 11º and pick up an 11º, a 15º, and an 11º. Go down the next 11º.

❹ Round 4 starts the adjustment to the spiral pattern. To begin, go up two 11ºs of the next stack, then pick up two 11ºs and go down two on the next stack. Come up only the top bead of the next stack. Follow the pattern for the rest of this side, going UP ONE, DOWN TWO around.

❺ For the last two rounds, pick up two 11ºs for each stitch (no 15ºs) and go UP ONE and DOWN ONE around. Work a normal step up.

❻ Simulate the look of a ladder after working the last two rounds by connecting the two-bead tall stacks as you would a ladder (**photo m**).

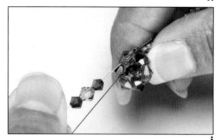

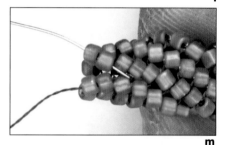

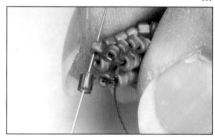

MATERIALS

- 22g Japanese seed beads, size 11º
- 5g seed beads, size 15º, accent color
- 33 4mm bicone crystals
- 9 5mm bicone crystals
- beading needles, #12 or #13
- Silamide or Nymo B beading thread
- clasp
- small number of matching cylinder beads for attaching clasp
- 2 3mm fire-polished beads or 8º seed beads to plug ends

FINAL TOUCHES

❶ Run your fingers over the centerpiece. If any of the crystals still feel loose or wobbly, use a new needle and thread to retrace the thread paths through the loose crystals.

❷ Use the thread at the end of the necklace if it is long enough or attach a new thread securely. String one of the 3mm plug beads and go down a stack on the opposite side of the row (**photo n**). Come back up the adjacent stack, go through the plug bead, and go down the stack next to the one from which you started. Repeat the thread path once or twice, but leave enough room in the plug bead so you can go through it several more times.

❸ Exiting the plug bead, pick up five to eight cylinder beads and one of the clasp parts. Position the clasp in the middle of the cylinder beads. Go through the plug bead and the cylinders several more times (**photo o**). End the thread in the rope.

❹ Repeat steps 2-3 on the other end.

Designed by Linda Lehman. Contact her at lehman_linda@hotmail.com or (301) 439-2679. To see more of her work, visit her website, emporiumofwearableart.com.

Tubes and spirals

Combine regular tubular herringbone with spiral herringbone for a bracelet that's sure to get noticed. This project begins with a removable bead ladder that was developed by Susan Hillyer. You're sure to find this a handy shortcut. Be aware that the larger you make a spiral tube, the flatter it becomes. Using various bead sizes helps it retain a ropelike appearance.

Construct this bracelet from the middle toward each end. The ends taper into a large spiral to which a button-and-loop clasp is attached. You might try inserting focal beads in the center spiral or substituting strands of beads for the center spiral and tubes.

MAKING THE FOUNDATIONS

❶ Begin by making a reusable ladder two beads high and 24 stitches long with the same kind of beads you'll be using for the project (see "Flat herringbone basics," p. 6). Use a contrasting color of beading thread or Fireline. Start the ladder by picking up four beads rather than two and change bead color after every ten stitches. After reinforcing the ladder, tie the starting and ending tails together with a surgeon's knot (see "Thread and knots," p. 4). Clip the tails. You'll use this ladder to start both sides of the bracelet.
❷ Place a stop bead 3-4 in. (7.6-10cm) from the end of a 1-2 yd. (.9-1.8m) length of beading thread by sewing through the bead twice.

❸ Row 1: To begin this row in herringbone, come up through the end pair of beads on the ladder, snugging the stop bead against the bottom of the ladder to help you maintain even tension. String two A beads and go down the second pair of ladder beads. Come back up the third pair (**photo a**, p. 34). Repeat until you have added 24 beads (12 stitches) and the needle is going down the last pair of ladder beads (**photo b**, p. 34).
❹ Join the row of herringbone into a ring by going up the first A bead strung. Make sure that the ladder is not twisted (**photo c**, p. 34).
❺ Row 2: Work tubular herringbone (see "Tubular herringbone basics," p. 22) around the circle with A: string two A, go down the second bead of row 1 and up the third. After adding the last two beads, work a normal step up by coming up the first two beads of the first stack. Snug up the stop bead (**photo d**, p. 34).
❻ To reinforce the join of the tube, go down the top bead of the last stack and come back up the top bead of the first stack (**photo e**, p. 34).
Row 3: Work in regular herringbone and MC, ending with a normal step up.
Row 4: The thread path of row 4 is unusual because it unifies the herringbone so that you can remove the ladder. Go down three and up three (all the herringbone beads in each stack) as you add pairs of MC beads. At the step up, go down three and come

up four (**photo f**, p. 34).
Row 5: Work in MC.
Row 6: Work the first six stitches as follows: 2MC; MC and B; B and C; C and B; B and MC; and 2MC. Repeat the pattern to complete the row.
Rows 7-9: Work as row 6.
Rows 10-12: Work in MC.
Rows 13-14: Work in A.
❼ To remove the ladder, loosen and remove the stop bead. Gently tug the herringbone beadwork away from the ladder as you carefully clip the threads that attach the ladder to the herringbone (**photo g**, p. 34). Remove any loose threads. If a long thread remains, leave it for later use.
❽ Make a second foundation piece as in steps 1-6. Do NOT remove the ladder.

MATERIALS

- 4 colors Japanese cylinder beads
  10g MC (main color—alabaster/purple)
  2g A (first accent color—pink/teal)
  3g B (second accent color—medium green/lavender)
  2g C (third accent color—chartreuse/ turquoise)
- 5g size 11º seed beads to match C (choose large Japanese 11º s or Czech 10º s)
- 2g size 14-15º seed beads to match A
- Nymo B or D beading thread
- beading needles #12 or 13
- 8mm bead or ½-in. (13mm) shank button

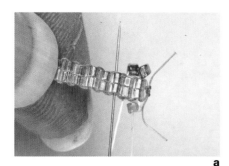

a

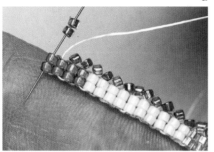

b

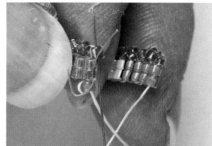

c

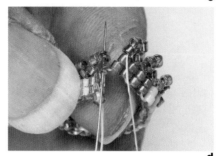

d

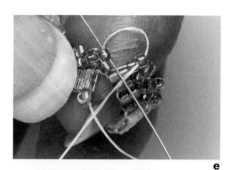

e

f

g

WEAVING THE SIDE TUBES

❶ Flatten the tube without the ladder so there are three stacks of MC on each side of the patterned section. The side tubes have four stitches around and are worked from the two outermost front and back stitches. Use the existing thread to begin the first side tube.

❷ For the first row, work the first two stitches in MC. Your needle will be going down the fourth stack of A in line with the first stack of the color pattern. Bring it up the A bead immediately behind the one it is exiting (**photo h**), pull snug, and work two MC stitches behind the first two stitches. The step up will be on the outer edge (**photo i**).

❸ Work the side tubes in the following color pattern:

Rows 1-3: MC.
Row 4: B.
Rows 5-7: MC.
Row 8: A.
Rows 9-11: MC.
Row 12: C.
Row 13: B.
Row 14: C.
Rows 15-17: MC.
Row 18: A.
Rows 19-21: MC.
Row 22: B.
Rows 23-25: MC.

❹ End the thread on this side tube.

❺ Add a new thread that exits the fourth stack in from the opposite edge (above the outer edge of the color pattern—**photo j**). Work rows 1-25 as in step 3. Leave the thread in place.

JOINING THE FOUNDATION PIECES

❶ Remove the ladder from the second foundation piece and flatten it so it has three stacks of MC on each side of the center pattern. You'll join the ladder end of this piece to the ends of the two side tubes.

❷ Use the thread exiting the side tube and go down two beads on the fourth stack of the foundation piece (**photo k**).

❸ Come up the two beads on the third stack from the edge and go down the matching two beads on the tube (**photo l**). Tighten the thread. Continue in this manner, joining the four stitches of the tube to the matching four stitches of the foundation.

❹ End by bringing the thread down the first two beads of the side tube and the top bead of the foundation.

❺ Zigzag through the next five beads on the middle section of the foundation, exiting the fourth bead from the edge (**photo m**). Join the other side tube, by repeating steps 1-4. When you are finished, the thread will exit the fourth bead from the edge on the foundation piece.

MAKING THE CENTER SPIRAL

To make the spiral, you first reduce the four stitches to three by placing a large 11º seed bead between the middle stacks on each side. The variety of bead sizes and the fact that you do not work regular herringbone (down one, up one) causes this tube to spiral. A little thread will show on the first few rows.

Row 1: As you add beads for each stitch, go down one then up two. Start by coming out the top bead on the fifth stack from the edge. For the first stitch, string an 11º, go down one and up two (**photo n**). Stitch 2 is two Bs (down one into the inside of the foundation on side 1, up two on the inside of side 2—**photo o**); stitch 3 is an 11º; stitch 4 is two 14ºs. For the step up, go down one and up three on the inside of the foundation (the third bead is the first 11º).

Row 2: Continue to go down one and up two. Stitch 1, 11º and B (**photo p**); stitch 2, B and 11º; stitch 3, two 14ºs and step up as before.

Row 3: Go down one and up two. First stitch, 11º and B; stitch 2, B and 11º; stitch 3, two 14ºs; end down one and up three.

Reinforcing row: Without adding beads, go down three and up four for the entire row until you exit the 11º in the first stack. As you work this row, ease any problem beads into proper alignment.

Row 4-31: For the rest of the spiral, the herringbone pattern is down one

h

i

j

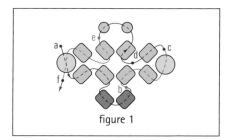

figure 1

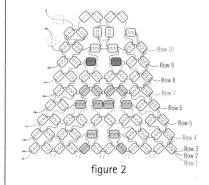

figure 2

k

l

m

n

o

p

and up three. There is no step up. Pull tight and the thread will no longer show.

CONNECTING THE SPIRAL

To make sure the spiral fits well, place the work on a flat surface. Don't twist the spiral. If it is too long or too short, remove or add rows.

❶ When the spiral is the right size, go down one and up two all the way around to pull the top together.

❷ You'll connect three beads on each side of the spiral to the four beads on each side of the center section of the foundation. With the thread exiting an 11º, go through the bead closest to the side tube and come out the next bead on the foundation. Go down the second spiral bead and up the third (**figure 1, a–b**). Go up the third foundation bead, down the fourth, and through the other 11º (**b–c**).

❸ Go up the foundation bead closest to the other side tube (**c–d**). Go down the next foundation bead then down and up the last two spiral beads (**d–e**). Go up the next foundation bead, down

the last, and through the first 11º again (**e–f**). End the thread.

TAPERING THE BRACELET ENDS

To keep the outer edges smooth, the decreases are made in the middle of each side. I used different colors so the decrease pattern is easier to see. Work in regular herringbone. See **figure 2** for the taper rows.

❶ Position the thread so it exits an edge bead. Follow the pattern exactly, keeping the decreases centered on each side. After working a row on the first side, turn the piece over and repeat on the other side. Then step up to the next row.

Row 1: (six stitches) 2MC; 2MC; A and MC; MC and A; 2MC; 2MC.

Row 2: (six stitches with a decrease between stitches 3 and 4) 2MC; 2MC; string a C between the two beads on the stitch below (a decrease). Repeat in reverse order.

Row 3: 2MC; 2MC; go through the first C, string 2MC, go through the second C and up the next MC; 2MC; 2MC.

Row 4: 2MC; decrease with 1A; 2A; decrease with 1A; 2MC.

Row 5: 2MC; go through the single A, string 2C, go through the pair of A, string 2C, then go through the single A and up the next MC; 2MC.

Row 6: 2MC four times. Note: six stitches have been reduced to four.

Row 7: 2MC; 1B; 1B; 2MC.

Row 8: 2MC; go through the first B, string 2MC, go through the second B, and come up the next MC; 2MC.

Row 9: On this row, the sides begin to

merge. String an MC, go down the next MC, and through the first horizontal MC; 2MC. Go through the second horizontal MC and up the next MC. String 2MC, go down the last MC on this side and up the first MC on the other side.

Row 10: Go through the horizontal MC, string 2MC, go down and up the next 2MC, string 2MC, go down and up the last 2MC on the side. Then go through the horizontal MC to work the two stitches on the other side.

2 Work the button end of the large spiral from this taper. Then repeat the taper on the other end and finish with a large spiral and loop.

MAKING THE LARGE SPIRAL

Row 1: Go down one and up one. For the first stitch, string an 11º and an MC. Stitch 2 is an MC and a 14º. Stitch 3 is an 11º and an MC. Stitch 4 is an MC and a B. Step up through two beads.

Row 2: Add the same beads as in row 1, but go down one and up two on each stitch; step up through three.

Rows 3-23: Follow the pattern but go down one and up three. There is no step up. Lengthen or shorten the end spirals to make the bracelet the desired length.

ADDING THE BUTTON

1 You need to taper the end spiral to add the button or 8mm bead.

Row 24: Go down one and up two and add one bead over each stitch as follows: 11º, MC, 11º, MC. You now have two stitches.

Rows 25-27: Go down one and up two. Stitch 1 is an 11º and an MC. Repeat for stitch 2. Close the spiral by going up one and down two around the last row.

2 Bring the needle down the spiral about six rows to add the button or bead. Position the needle so the closure will sit on the center top of the spiral.

3 Sew the button between two beads, repeating the thread path as many times as possible for security.

4 If you're using an 8mm bead instead of a button, position the needle as for the button. String an MC, the bead, an 11º, and a C. Go back down the 11º and the bead and string an MC. Go through the same or a neighboring bead on the spiral (**photo q**). Reinforce the thread

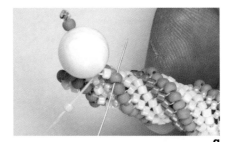

q

r

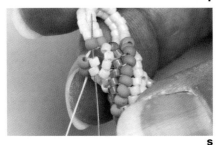

s

path as many times as possible.

5 End the thread and trim.

MAKING THE LOOP END

1 Repeat the taper on the other end of the bracelet.

2 Repeat the large spiral, working 26 rows or the number desired.

3 To form the loop, you work on only half the spiral. Row 1 reduces two stitches on one side of the large spiral into a long strip of 2MC.

Row 1: Go down one and up two (**figure 3, a–b**). Add an 11º and go down one (**b–c**). Come up two (**c–d**). Add an 11º and go down one (**d–e**). Come up two (**e–f**).

Row 2: 2MC, go down two, and up three including the step up (**figure 4, a–b**).

Row 3: 2MC, down three, and up four (**b–c**).

Row 4: 2MC, down two, and up three (**c–d**).

4 For an 8mm bead closure, repeat row 4 for a total of 15 rows. For a ½-in. (13mm) button, work a total of 20 rows.

5 Final row: add two 11º beads. Go down two and up three. Make sure the loop fits over the bead or button securely. Then reinforce the end, going

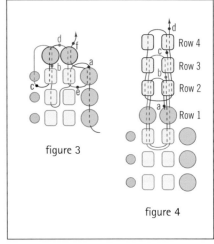

figure 3

figure 4

down two and up two.

6 To attach the loop to the other side of the spiral, go down the 2B and come up the adjacent 2MC beads.

7 Go back into the same 11º on the loop (**photo r**) and come down out of the other 11º.

8 Attach this 11º to the two free stacks on the second side of the spiral by going down the two 11ºs next to the first join and coming up the adjacent 2MC. Go back through the same 11º (**photo s**) and the bead above, then go down the stack with the first 11º. Sew the two MC stacks of the spiral together.

9 Reinforce the join and end the thread.

Designed by Lynn Bergman. Contact her at email at cleo@pacbell.net or in care of Kalmbach Publishing at books@kalmbach.com.

VARIATIONS & COMBINATIONS

Variation and combination basics

Combine herringbone with other stitches for textural variation.

BRICK STITCH

Brick stitch, also known as Comanche stitch, is usually started with a single row of beads known as a ladder (see "Flat herringbone basics," p. 6). Successive rows are added by stringing a bead and then stitching through the loops of thread that run between the beads on the previous row.

Begin each row so no thread shows on the edge: String two beads. Go under the thread between the second and third beads on the ladder from back to front. Pull tight. Go up the second bead added, then down the first. Come back up the second bead.

For the remaining stitches on each row, pick up one bead. Pass the needle under the next loop on the row below from back to front. Go back up the new bead.

INCREASING BRICK STITCH AT THE END OF A ROW

To increase at the start of a row, work as usual, but instead of going under the loop between the second and third beads, go under the loop between the first and second beads of the row below. Continue in regular brick stitch.

INCREASING BRICK STITCH WITHIN A ROW

To increase within a row, work as usual but attach the increase bead to the same loop that the previous bead is attached to.

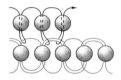

SQUARE STITCH

Square stitch, a durable weave in which beads are aligned neatly in both vertical and horizontal rows, is one of the easiest stitches to learn. Many beaders like to use square stitch as an alternative to loom weaving because it produces the same look without numerous threads that have to be finished off. Because square stitch produces a nice even grid, it is particularly well-suited to Japanese cylinder beads, Other bead types work fine as well, especially if an uneven texture is desired.

String the required number of beads for the first row. Next, string the first bead of the second row and go through the last bead of the first row and the bead just added in the same direction. The new bead sits on top of the old bead and the holes are parallel.

String the second bead of row 2 and go through the bead below it. Continue through the bead just added. Repeat this step for the entire row and add more rows in the same manner.

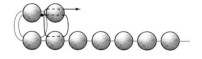

PEYOTE STITCH

Peyote stitch, sometimes referred to as gourd stitch, is a very popular and versatile weave that is adapted from traditional Native American beadwork. Today, peyote stitch is used in a wide variety of projects, from basic jewelry to complex, intricate sculptures.

EVEN-COUNT FLAT PEYOTE

String one bead and loop through it again in the same direction (remove the extra loop and weave the tail into the work after a few rows). String beads to total an even number.

Every other bead drops down half a space to form row 1. To begin row 3 (count rows diagonally—the numbers in the drawings below indicate rows), pick up a bead and stitch through the second bead from the end. Pick up a bead and go through the fourth bead from the end. Continue in this manner. End by going through the first bead strung.

To start row 4 and all other rows, pick up a bead and go through the last bead added on the previous row.

To end a thread, weave through the work in a zigzag path, tying half-hitch knots (see "Thread and Knots" p. 4)

along the way. Go through a few more beads before trimming the thread close to the work. To resume stitching, anchor a new thread in the work with half-hitch knots, zigzag through the work, and exit the last bead added in the same direction. Continue stitching where you left off.

EVEN-COUNT CIRCULAR PEYOTE
String an even number of beads to equal the desired circumference. Tie in a circle, leaving some ease.

Even-numbered beads form row 1 and odd numbered beads, row 2. (Numbers indicate rows.) Put the ring over a form if desired. Go through the first bead to the left of the knot. Pick up a bead (#1 of row 3), skip a bead and go through the next bead. Repeat around until you're back to the start.

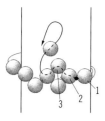

Since you started with an even number of beads, you need to work a "step up" to be in position for the next row. Go through the first beads on rows 2 and 3. Pick up a bead and go through the second bead of row 3; continue.

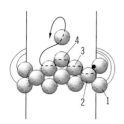

ODD-COUNT CIRCULAR PEYOTE
Start as for circular even-count steps 1–2 above. However, when you begin with an odd number of beads, there won't be a step up; you'll keep spiraling.

RIGHT-ANGLE WEAVE
Right-angle weave is so named because each bead sits at a right angle to its neighbors. The resulting bead fabric has a lovely drape and texture.

To begin, string four beads and tie them into a snug circle. Pass the needle through the first three beads again.

Pick up three beads and sew back through the last bead of the previous circle and first two new beads.

Continue adding three beads for each stitch until the first row is the desired length. You are sewing circles in a figure-8 pattern and alternating direction with each stitch.

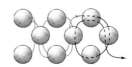

To begin row 2, sew through the last three beads of the last stitch on row 1, exiting the top bead of the stitch.

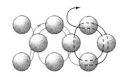

Pick up three beads and sew back through the bead you just exited and the first new bead, sewing in a clockwise direction.

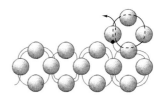

Pick up two beads and sew through the next top bead of the row below and the last bead of the previous stitch. Continue through the two new beads and the next top bead of the row below, sewing counter-clockwise.

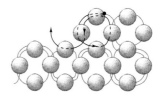

Sewing clockwise, pick up two beads, go through the side bead of the previous stitch, the top bead on the row below, and the first new bead. Keep the thread moving in a figure 8. Pick up two beads for the rest of the row.

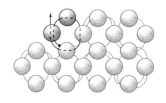

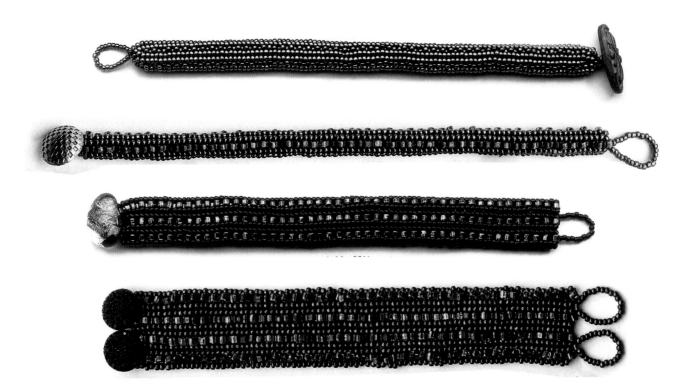

Triple herringbone

Herringbone usually is stitched two beads at a time, but why not try a three-bead variation? Triple herringbone is fairly simple, and the outcome is beautifully supple, whether you work it tubular or flat. Here are some of the possible variations with triple herringbone:

• Use a "big bead" (one size up from the beads on either side of it) in the middle.

• Use the same size bead throughout and work four sets of three for a boxlike effect. The beadwork retains the drapey feel of herringbone, but it also has enough firmness for a bangle.

TRIPLE TUBULAR HERRINGBONE – BRACELETS 1 & 2

❶ Start with 1-2 yd. (.9-1.8m) of single beading thread.

❷ Make a bead ladder in a three-bead repetition for the base row: String beads 1 and 2 and tie them together with a square knot (see "Thread and knots," p. 4). Leave about a 12-in. (31cm) tail for finishing the end later. Bring the needle up through bead 2, add bead 3 and *go up through bead 2 again. Come down through bead 3, pick up bead 4. Go down through bead 3 again and come up through bead 4. Pick up bead 5 and repeat from *. For a three three-bead set (bracelet 1, top bracelet, above) you will have nine beads. For a four three-bead set (bracelet 2, second from top) you will have 12 beads (figure 1).

❸ To make a circle, connect bead #1 to bead #12 of the ladder by going down bead #1 (figure 1, red line).

❹ Begin your first row of herringbone (if you are right-handed, work right to left; if you are left-handed, work left to right): Turn the ladder circle over so you are coming out the first bead of the first three-bead set. Pick up three beads. The second bead of this set will be the odd bead (bigger or a different color), and go down the third bead of the bead ladder beneath (figure 2). Go up the first bead of the next three-bead set and repeat.

❺ Work three-bead sets to the end of the row. Connect your last set to the first set of that row by going up the first bead in the first set on the previous row and the first bead of the first set of the row just worked (row 2) as shown in figure 3. This is the "step-up" to begin row 3.

❻ Continue making rows as shown in figures 2-3 for the desired length of the bracelet. I make most of my bracelets about 6¼ in. (16cm) long.

❼ Rather than make the end straight across, I draw it in by putting only one bead on top of each three-bead set. Then I sew through these four beads (on a 12-bead bracelet) several times. Next I attach one end of the closure (a button or toggle). Repeat this step on the other end for the other half of the clasp, using the long thread tail. This bracelet is about 7¼ in. (18.5cm) long.

To measure how big the loop needs to be to go over any button, string a bunch of beads onto the ending thread. It is a good idea to add more beads than you'll need. Bring the beads together in a loop and slip it over the button at the button's widest part. Move your fingers to within one bead of a perfect fit and drop off the extra beads. Always reinforce the closure joints by sewing through them multiple times.

RIGID TRIPLE TUBULAR HERRINGBONE – BRACELET 3

Bracelet 3 (third from top) has a base of six three-bead sets and is worked in a two-row repeated pattern. It is about 1¼ in. (3cm) wide and rigid. The look is somewhat open.

❶ Make the base row (ladder) the same as for bracelets 1 and 2. You will have 18 beads in this ladder.

❷ Work the two-row herringbone pattern as follows: Row 1 is one 11º, one 8º, and one 11º (**black line, figure 4**).

❸ Begin row 2 with the step up, but string one 11º, go into the 8º of the previous row, and string one 11º. Repeat around (**red line, figure 4**).

❹ Alternate rows 1 and 2 until the bracelet is long enough. Then finish the ends and attach the clasp as above.

TRIPLE FLAT HERRINGBONE – BRACELET 4

The bottom bracelet has four three-bead sets (12 beads). The bracelet is about 1½ in (4cm) wide. The interesting thing about flat triple herringbone stitch with a larger bead in the middle of each set is that if you use two different beads, alternating them every row, the large bead on every other row drops back. Turn your work over and this is the bead that pops forward, giving your bracelet a reversible look.

❶ Begin the flat bracelet with a ladder, but do not connect the first and last beads. With your thread coming up through the last bead, turn the work and pick up three beads for the second row.

❷ For a reversible look, use the second center bead color on the first triple herringbone row. Continue across as in figure 2.

❸ The row will end with the needle going down the last small bead on the previous row. To get your thread in the correct position to begin the next row (and every row after that), turn the work and go through the bead next to the one the needle is exiting (the middle bead). (Remember that holes of the two outside beads of a set are vertical, and the hole of the middle bead is horizontal.) Cross

over to the last bead of the row you just added and go up through it (**figure 5**). Pull the thread tight on the edge. Now string the first three-bead set of the next row. Continue in this manner until the bracelet is long enough.

❹ If you wish to stabilize the edge beads, run your thread vertically through every bead on each side. Because of the crossover at the beginning of every row, some beads tend to swing out more than others. This lines them up again.

❺ Use any type of closure you wish.

figure 1

figure 2

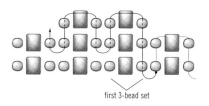

figure 3

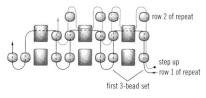

figure 4

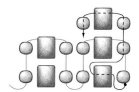

figure 5

MATERIALS

for all bracelets:
- #10 or 12 beading needle
- Nymo D or Silamide bead thread
- optional: Thread Heaven or beeswax

bracelet 1 (green and gold)
- size 11º seed beads:
  15g color 1
  15g color 2
- button

bracelet 2 (gold, transparent gold triangles)
- 15g 11º seed beads
- 10g size 8º seed beads or 10º triangle beads
- button

bracelet 3 (black and multi-colored)
- 15g size 11º seed beads
- 15g size 8º seed beads or 100 triangle beads
- 1–2 buttons

bracelet 4 (purple and blue)
- 15g size 11º seed beads
- 15g size 8º seed beads or 10º triangle beads
- 2–3 buttons

Designed by Donna L. Zaidenberg. Contact her via e-mail at donna.l.zaidenberg@us.hsbc.com.

VARIATIONS & COMBINATIONS

This colorful bag is a sampler of bead stitches. It begins with a row of circular ladder stitch in 3.3 cylinder beads followed by two rows of circular brick stitch. Then you work tubular herringbone stitch with 11º cylinder beads, following the chart on p. 44 from top to bottom. The bottom panel is worked flat on part of the tube, and the button flap contains a short section of right-angle weave. Use flat peyote stitch for the strap, or use a strand of beads strung on strong cord.

MAKING THE PURSE'S BODY

❶ Thread a needle with 4 yd. (3.6m) of Silamide. Weave a ladder with 36 size 3.3 beads (see "Flat herringbone basics," p. 6). Make sure the ladder isn't twisted and join it into a circle by going up the first bead, back down the last bead, and back up the first bead.

❷ Work two rows of brick stitch around the circle (see "Variation basics," p. 38). Join the first and last beads of each row as in the ladder.

❸ Coming up out of a brick stitch bead, begin row 1 of tubular herringbone stitch. Pick up two cream cylinder beads and sew back down the same 3.3 cylinder bead (**photo a** and **figure 1, a–b**). Tighten the thread so the 11º beads line up side by side on the 3.3 bead. Sew up the next 3.3 bead and repeat to add pairs of 11º beads over each 3.3 (**b–c**).

❹ Join the circle and step up to work the next herringbone row by coming up the first 3.3 and the first herringbone stitch bead of the previous row (**figure 2, a–b**).

❺ String two cream cylinder beads and go down the second bead in the first herringbone pair (**photo b**). Then come up the first bead in the next pair (**b–c**). Repeat around, ending with the needle going down the last herringbone bead of the previous row (**d**).

❻ From now on, work all step ups as follows: Go up the first bead of the row below the row just completed and the

Herringbone bag

first bead of the just completed row (figure 3, a–b). Pick up two beads and go down the second bead of the previous row and come up the next bead (b–c). When you need to end or add thread, do so just before stepping up so you don't get confused about which bead comes next. End thread by following the thread path and tying two or three half-hitch knots (see "Thread and knots," p. 4) between beads. Add thread the same way, but follow the thread path to end where you left off with the needle pointing the same way.

❼ Follow the graph on p. 44 to complete the 31 body rows of the purse.

MAKING AND CLOSING THE BOTTOM FLAP

❶ Sew through the beadwork to exit the bead on row 31 where the flap begins (figure 4, a–b). Stitch the first 32-bead flap row (b–c) Your thread is going down a bead on the previous body row. To turn and start the next flat row, go around the thread below the bead your needle is exiting. Then go up that bead and the last bead added (c–d). String two beads and work flat herringbone stitch to the end of the row. Repeat the turn as you begin each of the four flap rows.

❷ To join the flap to the other side of row 31, fold it over so there are four beads on the purse's bottom edge along each side of the flap. Sew down the fifth bead across from the flap bead your needle is exiting (photo c). Sew up the next bead on the purse's bottom edge and through the second bead on the flap's edge (photo d). Continue stitching between bead pairs on the purse and flap edges.

❸ When you reach the end of the flap row, stitch between the four beads along the flap's side and the four remaining beads on the bottom row. Finish the thread and trim the tail.

❹ Begin a new thread to join the flap's other side to the purse's bottom, repeating step 3.

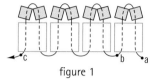

figure 1

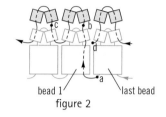

bead 1   last bead

figure 2

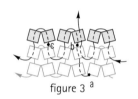

figure 3

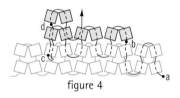

figure 4

MAKING THE BUTTON CLOSURE

❶ Lay the purse flat with the front facing you. There are 18 ladder-stitched 3.3 beads on the front and the back sides.

❷ Thread a needle with 2 ft. (61cm) of doubled Silamide and weave the thread securely into the brick-stitched beads on the front. Exit the ninth brick-stitch bead from one side edge on the row above the first row of cylinder beads. Pick up a cylinder bead and sew from back to front through one hole of the button. Sew front to back through the other hole, pick up a cylinder bead, and stitch through the tenth bead on the same brick-stitch row. Tighten and reinforce the button attachment several times. End the thread with half-hitches between beads.

❸ Turn the purse over. Thread a needle with 4 ft. (1.2m) of Silamide. Sew through the 3.3s to secure the thread

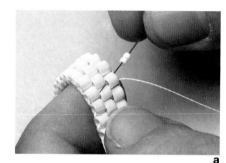

a

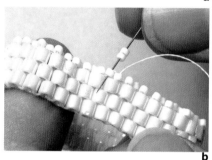

b

c

d

and exit bead #6 on the back top row. Add pairs of cream cylinder beads to beads #6-13 (figure 5, a–b, p. 44). Add two more rows of flat herringbone, working the turn as shown and explained in figure 4 and step 1 of making and closing the bottom flap.

❹ At the end of the third row, turn as if to start a new row, but sew through the last pair of beads (figure 6, a–b, p. 44). The beads will splay out and flatten.

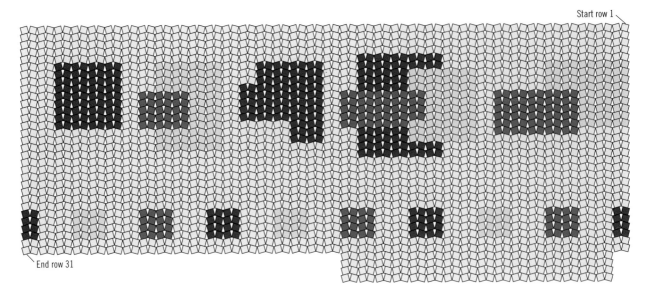

Start row 1

End row 31

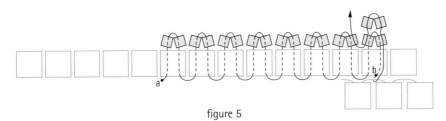

figure 5

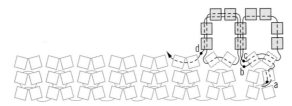

figure 6

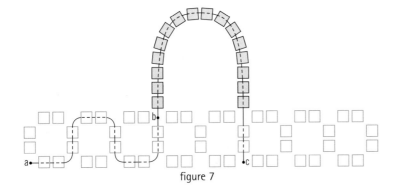

figure 7

❺ Work a row of eight-bead right-angle weave (see "Variation basics") across the herringbone row: Pick up six cylinder beads, and go back through the last pair of beads sewn through (**b–c**). Go through the first two beads added again and pick up four beads. Stitch back through the next herringbone pair, the last two beads of the previous stitch, and the four new beads (**c–d**). Add right-angle weave squares across the row of herringbone.

❻ Work two more rows of eight-bead right-angle weave.

❼ Sew back through the third row of right-angle weave so your needle exits the side between the third and fourth squares (**figure7, a–b**). Pick up enough cylinder beads to make a loop that will fit over the button. Sew down the side beads between the fifth and sixth squares (**b–c**). Reinforce the loop several times, then end the thread securely.

PURSE STRAP

The 23-in. (58cm) flat peyote (see "Variation basics") strap is attached to the back edge beads of the ladder. A simple strand of larger beads also works well. Reinforce the connections several times.

Designed by Isabee Demski. Contact her at (231) 832-0134 or 301 W. Lincoln Ave., Reed City, MI 49677.

MATERIALS
- 108 3.3 cylinder beads, cream
- Japanese cylinder beads, size 11º:
  15-20g matte cream
  7g each of red, yellow, and blue
- 1⅜-in. (1cm) two-hole button
- Silamide beading thread
- beading needles, #12 or 13

Embellished rope

The drape and flexibility of herringbone stitch provides a wonderful surface for all kinds of embellishment, including a trailing vine and branched fringe. After making a herringbone rope for the base of the necklace, stitch a traveling vine from one end to the other, adding leaf fringe to the vine as you go. Next add branch fringe to the rope. For balance, make the fringe denser and longer at the center of the necklace.

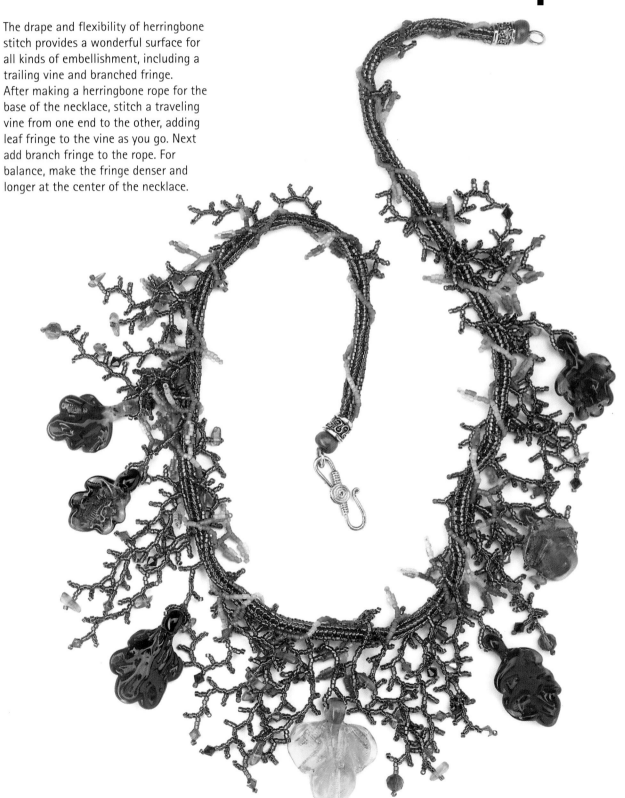

ROPE

❶ Leave an 8-in. (20cm) tail for finishing and string four main color (MC) cylinder beads. Go back through the four beads and pull the thread tight to make a square of two beads by two beads. Tie the tail and working thread in a square knot (see "Thread and knots," p. 4). Then go down the first two beads and up the second two beads (**figure 1, a–b**). String two beads. Go up the previous two and down the two new beads (**b–c**). String two beads, go down the previous two and up the two new (**c–d**). Repeat **b–d** for a total of six stacks.

❷ To join the six-stack ladder into a circle, start with the needle coming up out of the last two beads added. Go down the first two beads (**figure 2**). The thread exits in the opposite direction from the starting tail.

❸ Now you'll work herringbone stitch until the rope is the desired length. Your needle is exiting bead #1 on the ladder. Pick up two beads and sew up bead #2 toward the edge of the ladder and down (out) bead 3. Repeat twice more, adding a total of six beads, and end going up bead 6 (**figure 3, a–b**). To complete the first herringbone row and step up to begin the next row, come up bead #1 on the ladder and the first herringbone bead added (**b–d**).

❹ Work in herringbone until the rope is the desired length. Then stitch the last two rows of beads together as if they were a ladder so the end and the beginning of the rope are equally firm. Leave an 8-in. tail.

VINE AND LEAF FRINGE

❶ Start the vine with your needle exiting one of the ladder beads away from the rope (**figure 4, a**). String one vine-colored bead and go back through the end ladder bead in the same direction (**b–c**). Go back down the vine bead, which sits on top of the ladder bead (**c–d**). You have square stitched these two beads together.

❷ String seven vine beads and wrap them in the direction that you want the vine to travel. Square stitch the last bead to the rope, pulling the thread snug. You can attach anywhere, depending on how tightly you want the vine to spiral. I attach to every other column of herringbone, four to five beads below the last square stitch (**e–f**).

❸ As you add the vine, you also add the leaf fringe. After square stitching the seventh vine bead to the rope, string nine vine-color beads and five leaf-color beads (**figure 5, a–b**). Go back through the fourth leaf-color bead and string three more leaf-color beads (**b–c**). *Go back up three vine beads and string two vine beads. Make another leaf like the first and go through the next two vine-color beads (**c–e**). Repeat from * to make the last leaf fringe. End by going up the last three vine colored beads and the square-stitched vine bead (**e–f**).

❹ The number of leaf fringes you add to the vine can vary, depending on the desired thickness.

figure 1

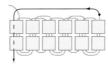

figure 2

figure 3

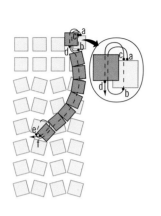

figure 4

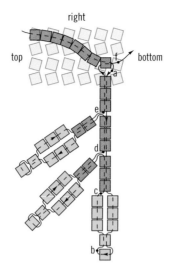

figure 5

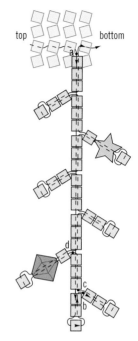

figure 6

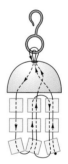

figure 7

BRANCHED FRINGE

The branched fringe is added directly to the herringbone rope after the vine and leaf fringes have been completed. You can make these fringes all the same length or graduate them from short at the ends to long at the center.

❶ Work the needle through a column of herringbone, coming out between vines. String 21 MC beads. Skip the last bead and go through the two above it (**figure 6, a–b**). String three beads, skip the last one, go through the first two (**b–c**).

❷ Continue up the main branch through the next three beads (**c–d**). Add three new beads. After you've added a branch or two, replace the second bead in some of the branches with a small accent bead or hang one of your larger accent beads from a looped branch.

❸ Vary the length of the branches by adding or subtracting three beads at a time from the initial 21.

❹ Continue adding branches along the same herringbone column until you reach the other end of the necklace. Then add branches along the next column. Work in this manner until the fringe is as thick as you wish. This necklace has branched fringe on three adjacent columns to keep the rope from twisting.

FINISHING TOUCH

❶ Thread the needle on one of the end tails. String a bead cap or a bead with a large enough hole to cover the end of the rope.

❷ Go through the loop on the clasp finding and back through the bead cap. Weave through two or three rows and back up to sew through the bead cap again (**figure 7**). Pass through the clasp loop and back through the bead cap. Repeat at least one more time to secure the join. Weave back through several more rows, tying half-hitch knots between the beads, and trim the thread. Dot the knots with glue.

❸ Repeat on the other end to connect the clasp's other half.

Designed by Lynn Larson. Contact her at 1435 4th St. SW, Huron, SD 57350 or llart@santel.net.

MATERIALS

- Japanese cylinder beads, size 11º
  30g main color
  10g each vine and leaf colors
- Nymo D to match main color beads
- beeswax or Thread Heaven
- beading needles, #10 or 12
- clasp
- assorted pressed glass beads and crystals to complement main colors, approx. 3-6mm:
  Swarovski crystals, Czech fire-polished beads, pressed glass bead shapes, triangle beads, cubes, gemstones
- 7-9 accent beads (lampworked leaves)
- 2 bead caps or large-hole metal beads
- G-S Hypo Cement

VARIATIONS

Floral herringbone

Herringbone flowers are simple to make and instantly gratifying. Here they are displayed on a delicate bracelet, but they also could be dangled at the ends of a beaded rope necklace, suspended as earrings, or sewn to a fabric picture frame for a personal touch.

SMALL FLOWER

Start these herringbone flowers with a ladder-stitch base. Then work increases between the herringbone stitches to form a trumpet-shaped flower. All rows end with a step up. Note: for clarity, larger beads were used in the photos.

1 Leaving a 6-in. (15cm) tail, start with 2 ft. (61cm) of conditioned purple Nymo. Use purple beads throughout.

2 Working with 15° seeds, make a bead ladder six beads long (see "Flat herringbone basics," p. 6). Join the ends to form a circle by going down the last bead strung (**photo a**). Go up the first bead and down the last bead again. With the tail and working thread, tie a surgeon's knot (see "Thread and knots," p. 4).

3 Sew up the first bead strung. Pick up two 15°s and go down the next bead. Go up the next bead (**photo b**). Repeat around the ladder and step up through the first beads strung in rows 1 and 2 (**photo c**).

4 Pick up two 15°s and go down the next 15°. String an 11° (**photo d**) to make an increase and go up the next 15°. Repeat around.

5 Using 15°s, work a herringbone stitch, then work an increase using two 11°s (**photo e**). Repeat around the tube.

6 Using 15°s, make another stitch. Come up the adjacent 11°. Work a stitch with two 11°s (**photo f**). Repeat around, working in the established bead sizes.

7 Repeat step 6 three more times. As you work, pull tightly to create the trumpet shape of the flower.

8 Tie off the working thread by weaving through several rows (**figure**) and tying half-hitch knots (see "Thread and knots") at points **a–d**. The thread tail will be used later.

9 Make another small flower.

LARGE FLOWER

Turn a small flower into a larger one by starting with a longer ladder and working additional increases to expand the size of the trumpet.

1 Starting with an eight-bead ladder of 15°s, follow steps 1–6 of the small flower.

2 Using 15°s, work a herringbone stitch. Pick up a 15° to work an increase. Do another stitch using 11°s. Then do an increase with a 15°. Repeat around the tube, working in the established bead sizes. End with a step up.

3 Using 15°s, work a herringbone stitch. Then pick up two 15°s to do an increase. Do a stitch in 11°s and increase with two more 15°s. Repeat around in the established pattern.

4 Repeat step 8 of the small flower.

ADD THE FLOWER STAMENS

Work inside each flower to make three stamens. Anchor a stamen through a single 11° at the flower's base.

1 Start with 2 ft. (60cm) of conditioned gold or yellow Nymo. Use yellow or gold beads.

2 Leaving a 3-in. (76mm) tail, sew into the flower and exit through one of the single 11°s near the base (**photo g**, p. 50). String eight cylinders and one 11° seed. Skip the 11° and sew back through the cylinders (**photo h**, p. 50). Exit the 11° flower bead from the opposite side entered.

3 Weave over to the next single 11° and repeat step 2 with the same or a varying number of beads. Repeat with the last 11°.

a

b

c

d

e

f

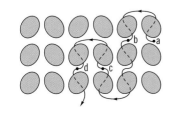

g

h

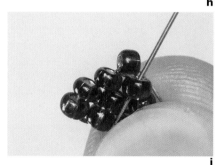

i

j

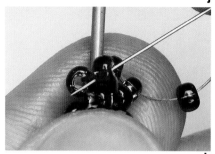

k

l

4 If desired, add more stamens to the large flower by working two stamens from one 11º.

5 Tie off the thread as in step 8 of the small flower.

SMALL LEAF

Make the leaves in brick stitch. Start with a row of ladder stitches, work one end of the leaf, then weave back to the base row and weave the other end. Each small flower has two leaves.

1 Leaving a 6-in. tail, start with 2 ft. of conditioned green Nymo. Use green 8º seeds to work the leaves.

2 Make a bead ladder four beads long. Work a three-bead row of brick stitch, then a two-bead row (see "Variation basics," p. 38). Pick up one bead. It will sit perpendicular to those in the other rows. Sew through the first bead in the last two-bead row of brick stitch (**photo i**).

3 Weave back to the ladder stitch row and exit the first bead strung. Work in brick stitch until two beads remain.

4 Attach the leaf to the base of a small flower. With the thread remaining from

the two-bead end of the leaf, zigzag between a bead on the leaf and a bead on the flower (**photo j**). Tie off the thread using half-hitch knots and weave the tail through several beads. Trim the ends.

5 Use the tail from the ladder stitch row to zigzag the side of the flower to the leaf so it doesn't flop.

6 Make and attach two small leaves for each small flower.

LARGE LEAF

1 Make an eight-bead ladder and repeat steps 1-6 of the small leaf.

2 Make and attach three large leaves.

MAKE THE PEYOTE BRACELET

Weave a simple strap for the bracelet by working a five-bead tube of odd-count peyote. Because of the small diameter of this tube, you may want to work the first few inches around a 1mm core such as an unfolded paper clip.

1 String five green 8ºs to begin odd-count tubular peyote (see "Variation basics"). Use a 1mm rod or needle for support, if desired. **Photo k** shows the

tube in process. Continue for 6½ in. (16.5cm). My finished bracelet is 7¾ in. (19.7cm) long. Adjust the length of the tube as needed to fit your wrist.

2 To make the loop clasp, string at least 36 seeds. Sew through one of the last beads in the tube (**photo l**). Measure to see that the loop will slip over the large flower. Retrace the thread path several times and anchor the thread tails in the tube. Tie off with half hitches, dab with glue, and trim the tails.

ATTACH THE FLOWERS

Attach the small flowers to the end of the loop (clasp) and the large flower to the other end of the tube.

1 Anchor a doubled length of green Nymo inside one of the small flowers. Sew through the flower into one of the seeds in last row of a leaf. At the center point of the beaded loop, sew around the main thread, then go back through the leaf seed.

2 Sew into a corresponding leaf seed on the other small flower. Zigzag between the two leaf seeds several times, sewing under and over the thread on the loop to secure the flowers to it. Weave into the second flower to tie off the tail as before.

3 Use the thread tail on the opposite end of the peyote tube to anchor the base of the large flower by zigzagging through seeds in the tube and the flower. Tie off the thread as before.

Designed by Samara Kaufman. Contact her at sammie_ammie@yahoo.com. To see more of her work, visit her website, geocities.com/equal_gurl/beads/.

Beaded garden

Make a one-of-a-kind necklace or brooch by stitching together a variety of interesting shapes. Shapes are a great way to play with stitches. When you have enough pieces, sew them together. Consider adding a beaded cabochon to highlight your design.

Work with about 60 in. (1.5m) of thread. Use Nymo O for the beaded

shapes because of the many thread passes, and use Nymo B for the strap.

FAN

Stitch the fans in two-bead brick stitch and modified herringbone. If you prefer to work in single-bead brick stitch, make twice as many rows.

① Make a ladder of six two-bead units

(see "Flat herringbone basics," p. 6).
② On the second row, use brick stitch to increase (see "Variation basics," p. 38) from six to nine stitches (**figure 1, a–b**, p. 53).
③ On the third row, increase to 12 stitches (**b–c**).
④ Work one row of herringbone across the fan base, going up and down through both beads in each stitch (**figure 2, a–b**, p. 53). To turn, come up the brick-stitch beads in the previous column, then jog over and come up the edge herringbone bead (**b–c**).
⑤ Work a second herringbone row across the fan (**c–d**) and turn as shown (**d–e**).
⑥ For the rest of the fan, pick up four beads for each herringbone stitch. To make the fan divide into "fingers," pick up a group of four beads and go down through the first herringbone row (**e–f**). Then come back up all the beads on the first side of the next stitch (**f–g**). Work across the row (**g–h**). Turn as shown (**h–i**).
⑦ Work two or three more rows as in step 6 (**i–j**).
⑧ Finish the fan by adding one bead at the top of each finger (**j–k**).

RUFFLED FAN
The ruffled fan has a longer brick-stitch section and a second herringbone layer.
① Start with a ladder of four beads.
② Work three brick-stitch rows, increasing to five beads in the first row, six in the second, and seven in the third (**figure 3, a–b**, p. 53).
③ Work five two-bead rows, increasing to eight stitches in the first, nine in the second, 12 in the third, 16 in the fourth, and 20 in the fifth (**b–c**).
④ Finish the brick stitch section with a row of 20 single-bead stitches (**c–d**).
⑤ Work one row of herringbone across the previous row (**figure 4, a–b**, p. 53).
⑥ Work the next four rows in four-bead-per-stitch herringbone as in step 6 of the fan (**b–c**).
⑦ Finish the fan with a single bead at the top of each finger (**c–d**).
⑧ To make the ruffle, refer back to **figure 3** and start a new thread as shown. Then refer to **figure 5**, p. 53, and work a row of two-bead herringbone, as in step 4 of the fan (**a–b**), coming out in front of the 16-stitch row.
⑨ Work the next three rows in

four-bead-per-stitch herringbone as in step 6 (**b–c**).

10 End as in step 7 (**c–d**).

LARGE LEAF

1 Stitch a ladder alternating one bugle bead with a stack of three seed beads until you have five bugles and four stacks of seed beads (**figure 6, a–b**).

2 Square stitch (see "Variation basics") two rows of beads onto the ladder (**b–c**).

3 On the next row, begin brick stitching and decrease to eight stitches as follows: bugle, seeds, bugle, seeds, seeds, bugle, seeds, bugle (**c–d**).

4 Work the next seven rows in brick stitch as shown (**d–e**).

5 Go down through the bugles along the outer edge of the leaf and exit the edge ladder bugle (**e–f**).

6 Work the bottom five rows in brick stitch as shown (**f–g**).

7 Join the last bugle to the first on the end row to form a tube. End by coming back down the last bugle (**g–h**).

SMALL LEAF

The small leaf is similar to the large leaf in its shape and construction. Stitch the small leaf in brick stitch as shown in **figure 7**, p. 54, referring to the leaf instructions above, if necessary.

TWIG

1 Start with a four-bead ladder and join the ends to form a ring.

2 Work four rows of tubular herringbone (see "Tubular herringbone basics," p. 22) for a total of five rows (**figure 8, a–b**, p. 54). The fifth row is the base row.

3 Use the same technique as in the fan instructions to make two herringbone fingers (shown in red), going back down to the base row for each round. Make these fingers six to eight rows long and finish each with a single bead as before.

4 At this point, you are exiting the

MATERIALS

- seed beads, sizes 11º and 14º
- bugle beads, 4mm
- accent beads: shell heishi, 5-6mm and 3-4mm button-shaped freshwater pearls
- beading needles, #12 or 13
- Nymo beading thread, size O and B

bottom of the last bead in the base row again. Go up the first bead in the base row and work five rows of tubular herringbone (**c–d**). The fifth row in this group is the new base row.

5 Work another pair of fingers off the new base row as in step 3 (shown in blue).

6 Repeat steps 4-5, completing four sets of fingers.

LARGE FLOWER

1 Start with a six-bead ladder and join it into a ring (**figure 9, a–b**, p. 54). Work two rows of tubular herringbone (**b–c**).

2 Work the first part of an increase on the next row: Pick up two beads and go down the next column to make the first herringbone stitch, pick up one bead, and come up the next column (**c–d**). Repeat around, adding one bead between each stitch for a total increase of three beads (**d–e**).

3 Work the second part of the increase on the next row by picking up two beads where you picked up one on the previous row (**e–f**). Complete the row with three increases (**f–g**). You now have enough beads to make six herringbone stitches. This is the base row.

4 Make fingers five to six rows tall attached at the base as before (**g–h** shows two rounds). If you wish, you can work the last row or two by adding four beads per stitch as in the fan rather than two. Finish with a single bead at the top of each finger.

SMALL FLOWER

Use size 14º seed beads.

1 String ten beads and tie them into a circle with a surgeon's knot (see "Thread and knots"). Go through the first bead again.

2 Pick up two beads, skip one, and go through the next. Repeat around the circle. End by going through the first bead on the circle and the first bead of the first row (**figure 10, a–b**, p. 54).

3 Work two rounds of herringbone on the pairs of beads added in the previous round (**b–c**).

4 Increase one bead between each herringbone stitch on each of the next two rounds (**c–d**).

5 Work the next round in herringbone, going through the increase bead on the previous row (**d–e**).

6 Complete the short fingers with a single bead above each of the herringbone stitches. Work down through two beads and the increase bead as before (**e–f**).

ZIGZAG

1 String four beads and tie them into a circle. Go through the first two beads again (**figure 11, a–b**, p. 54).

2 Pick up two beads and go through the third bead on the circle (**b–c**).

3 Come back through the second bead and the first bead added (**c–d**).

4 Pick up two beads, go down the second bead of step 2, and come back up the first bead of step 2 and the first new bead (**d–e**).

5 Repeat step 4 until you've added six more rows (**e–f**).

6 Pick up one bead and go down the second bead on the row below and up the first (**f–g**).

7 To angle off, pick up two beads and go back through the single bead (**g–h**).

8 Pick up two beads, skip the single bead, and come out the second bead added in step 7 (**h–i**). Go down the first bead added in step 7 and the first bead added before the single bead. Come up the adjacent bead, through the single bead and the second bead added in step 7 (**i–j**).

9 Repeat steps 5-8 until you've made five to seven angled sections, ending with step 5.

10 End the last section by stringing a pearl and a size 14º and go back through the pearl. Continue down the other side of the section (**figure 12, a–b**, p. 54).

11 To embellish the angles, sew down then up the last two beads of the previous section, and through the single bead (**b–c**). Go up the bead next to the new section on the two-bead corner, string a pearl and a 14º, and go down the other corner bead (**c–d**). Continue down the side of the previous section (**d–e**).

SPIRAL

The spiral uses flat even- and odd-count peyote stitch (see "Variation basics") and brick stitch. Pull the thread tight as you work so the outer edge curls under.

1 String four beads and work two or three rows of even-count flat peyote stitch (**figure 13, a–b**, p. 54).

2 Pick up two beads for the first stitch

FAN

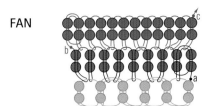

figure 1

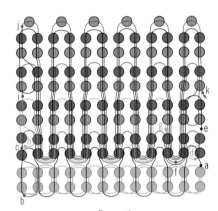

figure 2

RUFFLED FAN

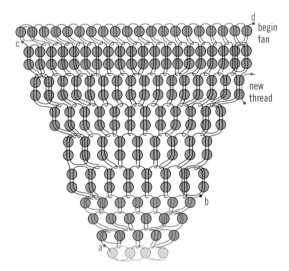

figure 3

LARGE LEAF

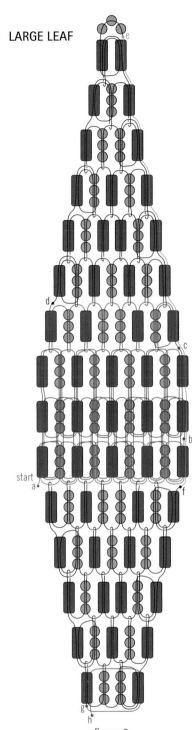

figure 6

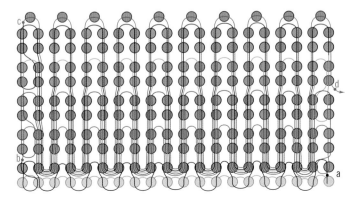

figure 4

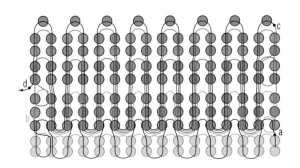

figure 5

SMALL LEAF

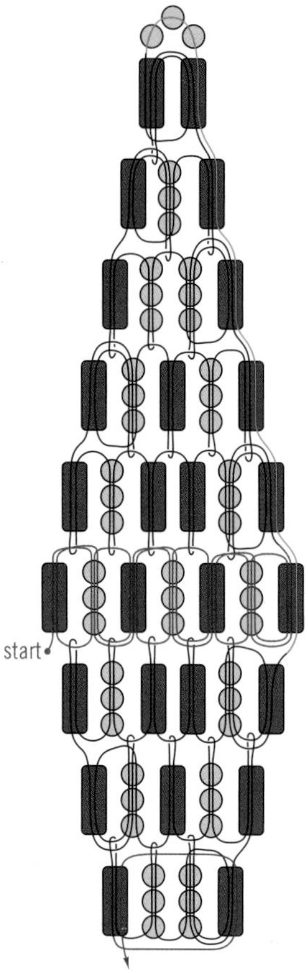

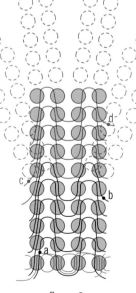

figure 7

LARGE FLOWER

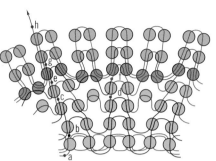

figure 9

SMALL FLOWER

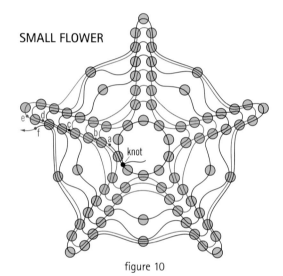

figure 10

SPIRAL

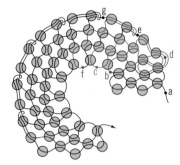

figure 13

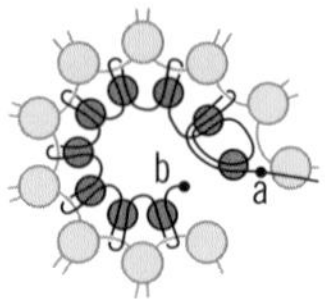

figure 14

PEARL-STUDDED ROPE

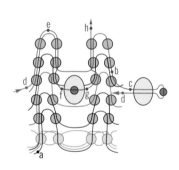

figure 15

TWIG

figure 8

ZIGZAG

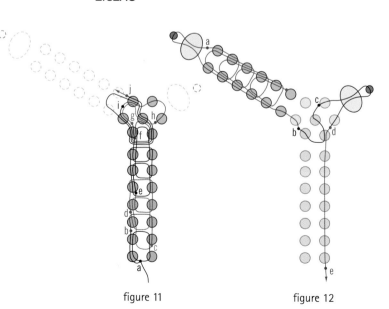

figure 11

figure 12

of the next row and make one more stitch. Peyote back toward the two beads, go through the first, pick up a bead, and go through the second (b–c).

❸ On this row, you change from even- to odd-count peyote. Pick up two beads and go through the last bead added on the row before. Add one bead each in the next two spaces (c–d). Then work the modified turn as shown (d–e).

❹ Work across the row, putting the third bead between the two beads at the start of the previous row (e–f). Work the next row, ending with a loop turn (f–g).

❺ Repeat steps 3-4 until the spiral is about two complete revolutions or as long as you wish. You can work the modified turn shown in step 3 or the loop turn in step 4.

❻ Bring the thread out the first peyote stitch bead on the inside edge of the spiral (figure 14, a). For a small spiral, work a row of brick stitch, using size 14ºs, along the thread loops on the inner edge (a–b). For a large spiral, work one row of brick stitch with 11ºs and one with 14ºs.

❼ Finally, sew the top of the brick stitch row to the outer edge of the spiral to maintain its shape. If desired, trim the spiral with two- to three-bead spiked fringe.

PEARL-STUDDED ROPE

❶ Start the rope with a four-bead ladder joined into a ring as in the twig.

❷ Work in herringbone to three or four rows past where you want the first pearls to be (figure 15, a–b).

❸ Continue down the column to the first pearl's location (b–c).

❹ String a pearl and a 14º. Go back through the pearl (c–d) and come up the next column to the top (d–e).

❺ Go down the next column. Exit the same row as for the first pearl (e–f).

❻ String the second pearl and seed bead and go back through the pearl (f–g). Come up the next column to the top (g–h) and resume the herringbone tube.

❼ Place pearls at regular intervals, repeating from step 2.

Designed by Lisa Olson Tune. Contact her at tunebdbdbd@aol.com.

Fan

Large flower

Ruffled fan

Small flower

Large leaf

Zigzag

Small leaf

Spiral

Twig

Pearl-studded rope

TIPS AND TECHNIQUES

Color wheel

Use a color wheel, like the simple one shown here, if you want help choosing colors for your beading projects. More complex color wheels can be found at art supply and craft stores as well as various websites. Besides the basic primary (red, blue, and yellow) and secondary (violet, green, and orange) colors shown here, some wheels show a full range of tints, shades, and hues. These can be helpful for choosing complementary (colors opposite each other) as well as analogous (colors adjacent to each other) color schemes.

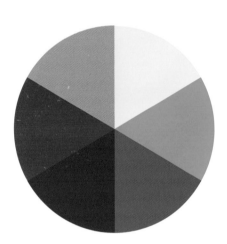

Herringbone tips

EASY HERRINGBONE START

As a beading teacher, I am always looking for ways to simplify difficult or complicated techniques for my students. Here's what I came up with to make the first rows of Ndebele herringbone stitch an easier task.

Figure 1

String four beads following the bead and color sequence in your design, then go through the beads again in the same direction (figure 1). String four more beads and go through them a second time (figure 2). Continue across the row, allowing about half a bead's width of space between groups. If you're working in flat herringbone, turn, pick up two beads, and stitch back across the row (row 3) following the directions for your project. If you're working a circular design, go down the first bead strung and up the bead next to it to complete the circle. String two beads to start row 3 and continue.

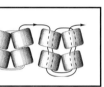
Figure 2

– *Cheryl Lawson, Washougal, WA*

MODIFIED HERRINGBONE

Pick up four beads instead of two when working flat or tubular herringbone, and you'll complete the piece in half the time. Attach each row to the bead below on the previous row as you normally would.

– *B.J. Guderian, Colville, WA*

NEW HERRINGBONE START

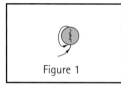
Figure 1

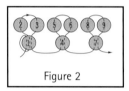
Figure 2

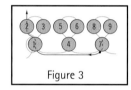
Figure 3

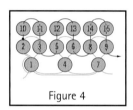
Figure 4

Here's an easy herringbone start:
Figure 1: Go through the first bead twice as a stop bead.
Figure 2: Exiting the top of the first bead, string two beads and go back down the first bead. String three beads, go back down the fourth bead. Repeat for the desired width.
Figure 3: To join the ends into a circle, go back up the first and second bead.
Figure 4: Now work regular herringbone: string two beads and go down the third bead and up the fifth bead. The single beads at the bottom pull together to close the end of the tube.

– *Huguette Coumbassa, Saint-Denis, France*